STORIES FROM A TEAROOM WINDOW

1 *(Frontispiece)*. The quiet setting of a tea cottage *(right)*, with the waiting bench in the outer part of the tea garden.

STORIES FROM A TEAROOM WINDOW

LORE AND LEGENDS OF THE
JAPANESE TEA CEREMONY

by Shigenori Chikmatsu
translated by Kozaburo Mori
edited by Toshiko Mori

TUTTLE PUBLISHING
Tokyo • Rutland, Vermont • Singapore

Published by Tuttle Publishing, an imprint of Periplus Editions (HK) Ltd., with editorial offices at 364 Innovation Drive, North Clarendon, Vermont 05759 USA and 61 Tai Seng Avenue, #02-12, Singapore 534167

© 1982 by Charles E. Tuttle Co., Inc.

All rights reserved.
No part of this publication may be reproduced, stored in a retrieval system or transmitted in any form or by any means, electronic, mechanical, photocopying, recording, or otherwise, without prior written permission from the copyright owner.

Library of Congress Catalog Card No. 82-80013
Previously published under ISBN 0-8048-1385-X

ISBN 978-4-8053-1063-2

Distributed by

North America, Latin America & Europe
Tuttle Publishing
364 Innovation Drive
North Clarendon, VT 05759-9436 U.S.A.
Tel: 1 (802) 773-8930; Fax: 1 (802) 773-6993
info@tuttlepublishing.com
www.tuttlepublishing.com

Japan
Tuttle Publishing
Yaekari Building, 3rd Floor
5-4-12 Osaki
Shinagawa-ku
Tokyo 141 0032
Tel: (81) 03 5437-0171; Fax: (81) 03 5437-0755
tuttle-sales@gol.com

Asia Pacific
Berkeley Books Pte. Ltd.
61 Tai Seng Avenue, #02-12
Singapore 534167
Tel: (65) 6280-1330; Fax: (65) 6280-6290
inquiries@periplus.com.sg
www.periplus.com

12 11 10 09   10 9 8 7 6 5 4 3 2 1

Printed in Singapore

TUTTLE PUBLISHING® is a registered trademark of Tuttle Publishing, a division of Periplus Editions (HK) Ltd.

Table of Contents

List of Illustrations	7
Translator's Preface	9
Introduction	13
Foreword to the 1804 Edition	21
Part One: Stories 1–113	23
Part Two: Stories 114–129	163
Afterword to the 1804 Edition	183
Glossary-Index	185

List of Illustrations

1 *(Frontispiece)*. View of a tea garden	
2. Plan of a four-and-a-half-mat room	26
3. Tea utensils arranged on a stand *(daisu)*	29
4. Ceramic tea caddy and its bag	30
5. Oil lampstand *(tankei)*	31
6. Kettles: *ubaguchi, tetori-gama,* Amida-do	35
7. Otogoze kettle	36
8. "The Hot Temper of Hideyoshi"	38–39
9. Flower containers: *shakuhachi* and Onjoji	42
10. Tearoom, showing the guest entrance *(kuguriguchi)*	47
11. Interior of a tearoom	49
12. Tea-leaf jar *(chatsubo)*	53
13. Kettle and brazier on a board *(koita)*	55
14. Lacquer tea caddies: *natsume* and *oshiroidoki*	58
15. Charcoal and charcoal containers	60
16. "Sweeping the Garden"	64–65
17. Ceramic tea caddies: *katatsuki, nasu,* and *utsumi*	71
18. Tea utensils arranged in the kitchen	75
19. *Efugo* water-vessel	82
20. Kettle rings	84
21. *Chakin*, tea scoop, and whisk	87
22. Rikyu's flower arrangements	92

23.	*Temmoku* tea bowl on stand *(temmoku-dai)*	99
24.	Bamboo flower-containers	101
25.	"The Gourd Flower-Container"	102–103
26.	Garden stone-basin and ladle	105
27.	Lacquer tea caddies: *mentori* and *seppu*	109
28.	Tea-whisk holder	113
29.	Tea scoops	115
30.	Selection of kettle-lid rests	117
31.	Ido tea bowl	122
32.	"Rikyu's Daughter"	128–29
33.	Stone lantern	134
34.	Stones by the garden basin	143
35.	Pothangers, kettle-ring hangers, and trivets	147
36.	*Imogashira* fresh-water jar	148
37.	Raku tea bowl	149
38.	"Sword-Sheath Design"	154–55
39.	Chrysanthemum and water *(kikusui)* crest-design	166
40.	"Lord Ryozan"	172–73
41.	Sealed tea-leaf jar	182

Translator's Preface

It was in 1973 that Toshiko Mori, my wife, came upon an old handwritten Japanese manuscript of this book in a pile of ancient documents in the Tokushima Prefectural Library. She was attracted by the stories it contained, and after further research she discovered that the book had been very popular among aficionados of the tea ceremony when it was first published in 1804. Her interest inspired her to produce a newly edited and annotated edition, which was published in 1978, exactly two hundred years after the death of the author, Chikamatsu Shigenori.

During the book's preparation I was able to observe my wife's work, sometimes discussing its content and sometimes enjoying a bowl of tea over it with her. Thus I came to attempt this translation into English.

Several features of the book have been adapted to make it easier for the Western reader to understand.

For example, Western dates and measurements have been added, and Shigenori's sometimes confusing use of names has been adjusted somewhat. It should be noted that people's ages are given in the stories by the Japanese count, which is one or two years greater than the equivalent Western count.

My happiness will be beyond description if these stories prove to be of interest to foreign readers, and help them to achieve a better understanding of the tea ceremony and of Japanese culture.

I would like to express my gratitude to Mr. R. P. Chase for his assistance in polishing this translation, and to Mr. Makoto Ando for help with the romanization of Chinese names. Thanks are also due to Mr. Hiroichi Tsutsui, director of the Urasenke Foundation's Konnichian Library, for his encouragement and assistance.

The Konnichian Library kindly allowed me to reproduce here illustrations from its copy of the 1804 *Chaso Kanwa (Stories from a Tearoom Window)*, which appear as Figs. 8, 16, 25, 32, 38, and 40. The National Diet Library permitted me to use Figs. 1, 3, 15, 21, 34, and 35, which come from the 1771 book *Chado Hayagaten (A Beginner's Guidebook to the Tea Ceremony)* by Chin'a. Figs. 2, 18, and 22 are from *Cha-no-yu: The Japanese Tea Ceremony* by A. L. Sadler, courtesy of the Charles E. Tuttle Company. The other illustrations are by the skilled hands of Fumiaka Kamada and Hide Doki.

I am indebted to the following works for information on the tea ceremony:

Hayashiya, Tatsusaburo, and Nagashima, Fukutaro. *Zusetsu Sado Taikei (Complete Illustrated Explanation of the Tea Ceremony)*. Tokyo: Kadokawa, 1963.
Iguchi, Kaisen. *Tea Ceremony*. Translated by John Clark. Osaka: Hoikusha, 1975.
Kuwata, Tadachika. *Sado Jiten (Dictionary of the Tea Ceremony)*. Tokyo: Tokyodo, 1956.
Okakura, Kakuzo. *The Book of Tea*. 1906. Reprint. Rutland and Tokyo: Charles E. Tuttle Co., 1956.
Sadler, A. L. *Cha-no-yu: The Japanese Tea Ceremony*. 1933. Reprint. Rutland and Tokyo: Charles E. Tuttle Co., 1963.
Yukawa, Sei. *Rikyu no Hana (Rikyu's Flowers)*. Tokyo: Tokyodo, 1970.

Note: In this book, premodern Japanese names are written in Japanese style (surname first), and modern names are written in Western style (surname last); however, the author's name is written in Western style on the jacket and title page.

Page references in italics refer to illustrations while those in roman refer to the text.

Introduction

CHIKAMATSU SHIGENORI, the author of this book, was born in 1695 the eldest son of Chikamatsu Shigekiyo, a warrior and retainer of the Tokugawa clan in Owari Province (Aichi Prefecture at present). Shigenori was commonly known as Hikonoshin, and he used the pen names Nankai and Nogenshi. He also signed his name Chikamatsu Hikonoshin Fujiwara Shigenori.

When Shigenori was seventeen, he was appointed page to the feudal lord of Owari. He was a very promising retainer and was expected to become a high councillor to the lord in the future. But when Shigenori had served in his post for only half a year, his lord died. After the late lord's brother succeeded him, Shigenori was put in charge of the horses and grooms, at a reduced salary. However, he was not discouraged by his demotion, but rather took advantage of his leisure time to study military science very diligently. In this way he was able to become an authority on military strategy, about which he wrote a hundred books. A versatile man, he also studied the tea ceremony, the Shinto religion, *haiku* poetry, and *waka* poetry.

Shigenori was not a professional tea master, but rather a warrior who studied and deeply enjoyed the tea ceremony. In 1739, he compiled a manuscript on the tea ceremony with the title *Chanoyu Kojidan (Legends of the Tea Ceremony)*. It consisted of seven volumes containing a total of three hundred five stories and anecdotes. However, Shigenori died in 1778, at the age of eighty-three, without seeing his work published.

The manuscript lay neglected until someone anonymously selected one hundred twenty-nine of the stories, revised them, and published them in 1804 under the title *Chaso Kanwa (Stories from a Tearoom Window)*. This book consisted of three volumes containing Stories 1–62, 63–111, and 112–129, respectively. Thus Shigenori's work was finally published, sixty-five years after its compilation and twenty-six years after the author's death. A second edition was published in 1816.

THE ORIGINAL INTRODUCTIONS

In coming to an understanding of the book and its author, one may turn to Shigenori's own words of introduction. He expressed himself in four propositions found in *Legends of the Tea Ceremony*:

茶窓閒話

1. This book was written about things I saw or heard tell of twenty years ago. There may be not a few mishearings or misunderstandings, but I have had no opportunity to correct any possible errors. Everything was written down from memory, so readers may come across mistakes.
2. The contents consist entirely of old stories told by tea masters or well-known anecdotes passed on from old. What is current and prevalent in present-day society is not contained here. This should be kept firmly in mind when reading this book.
3. The prices of various articles are presented in this book. It may seem a little too commercial for a warrior to be involved in such matters. But even in transactions dealing with swords, helmets, or other arms, the appropriate prices are decided after careful study and evaluation by the people concerned. Thus comments on the prices of articles cannot be done without. I sincerely ask my readers not to laugh at me for discussing such ignoble things as money and prices, even though I am a warrior.
4. I have been fond of the tea ceremony since childhood. I learned the tea ceremony at a Sen

school, and even though I have been busy with working hard at my profession of military science, I have enjoyed a bowl of tea whenever I could find time to spare. But under the circumstances, I could hardly make a thorough study of the rules and principles of the tea ceremony. When I think of the profound knowledge and achievement of many tea masters, I must address my sincerest apologies to my readers for my poor knowledge.

Despite Shigenori's modesty, the publication of his work was greeted with the utmost interest. Perhaps a better estimate of its significance is given in the original foreword to *Legends of the Tea Ceremony*. This was written in 1731 by Kobayashi Shisso, a man of Kyoto, who stayed with Shigenori for some time in order to write it. Shisso's comments illuminate Shigenori's true purposes, as well as the state of the tea ceremony at the time:

> It is a happy thing that the tea ceremony has become so very popular. When lords and leaders devote themselves to the tea ceremony, their retainers and followers are liable to indulge in it even more wholeheartedy. At present, all distinguished people are very fond of the tea ceremony, but regrettably they are liable to be too particular in regard to details or mere technique, and also to be

overly extravagant. Opposing this tendency, Chikamatsu Shigenori has written this book for a number of his disciples in the midst of his busy life as an instructor of strategy and military science. His sole desire is to convey an understanding of the true principles of the tea ceremony to tea aficionados. He hopes that this book may serve as a guiding light for those who practice the tea ceremony.

THE TEA CEREMONY AND ITS DEVELOPMENT

Stories from a Tearoom Window draws on a tradition that was centuries old even in Shigenori's day. Though tea was brought to Japan from China in a still earlier era, the classic Japanese tea ceremony was formulated by Murata Shuko in the fifteenth century. Shuko and Nakao Shinno (Noami) introduced this tea ceremony to the former shogun Ashikaga Yoshimasa, who, during a period of civil war and turmoil, found consolation in aesthetic pursuits at Higashiyama in Kyoto. In the sixteenth century, the tea ritual was further developed by Takeno Jo-o of Sakai near Osaka, where the prosperous merchants embraced it. The way of tea was perfected by Jo-o's disciple Sen no Rikyu, the greatest of all tea masters. Sponsored by the powerful warlords Oda Nobunaga and Toyotomi Hideyoshi, who were forcibly reunifying Japan, Rikyu established simplicity as the central element of the tea ritual. It was to the ideal of Rikyu that Shigenori wished to restore the tea ceremony (which he felt was falling into rigidity and extravagance) by compiling tales of earlier and "purer" ages.

The tea ceremony, Rikyu said, is nothing more than preparing and serving a bowl of tea. It is characteristic of Japanese culture, under the influence of Zen Buddhism, to find artistic and spiritual meaning in the commonplaces of daily life. Thus the arranging of flowers is considered an art form, and the preparation of a bowl of tea can express the essence of aestheticism. In the words of Kakuzo Okakura, the tea ceremony "is a cult founded on the adoration of the beautiful among the sordid facts of everyday existence. It inculcates purity and harmony, the mystery of mutual charity, the romanticism of the social order."

Drawn from daily life, the tea ceremony was refined to a point of great stylization. Every movement is prescribed, but this severe discipline gives rise to natural, harmonious action and total awareness of the moment. This Zen principle popularized the tea ceremony among feudal lords and warriors such as Shigenori, who sought the same thing in the military arts.

Before the guests arrive to take part in the tea ceremony, the host must make painstaking preparations. The tearoom and garden are carefully cleaned. A charcoal fire is built in the hearth or brazier and a kettle is put on to boil. With attention to the season and other aesthetic considerations, appropriate flowers, calligraphy, or other decorations are selected for the alcove. All is meticulously planned to produce an atmosphere of artless nature and tranquility.

The guests approach through the modest garden, which reflects the unaffected beauty of a mountain pass. After rinsing their hands and mouths at a stone basin, they enter the tearoom, a small and unpretentious hut. As they pass through its small doorway one by one, the guests must lower their heads, stimulating feelings of humility and of entering a serene new world.

When the guests have appreciated the decorations in the alcove and taken their places on the *tatami* mats, the host greets them and brings in the tea utensils from the kitchen. In a simple tea ceremony such as that described below, these consist of a fresh-water vesscl, tea bowl, whisk, tea scoop, tea caddy, ladle, waste-water vessel, and kettle-lid rest. Ceremoniously the host cleans the utensils, then scoops powdered tea from the caddy and places it in the tea bowl. He ladles hot water from the kettle into the bowl and whisks it into frothy green tea. In the case of *usucha* (thin tea), the first guest drinks the entire contents of the bowl, which the host then washes and refills with tea for the next guest. The kettle is replenished from the fresh-water vessel, while water used for cleaning goes into the waste-water vessel. In the case of *koicha* (thick tea), the bowl is passed from guest to guest, each taking a sip. When all the guests have been served, some of the utensils are presented to them for appreciation. The host removes the utensils and bows to the guests, marking the end of the tea ceremony. In more elaborate tea gatherings, a meal may be eaten and both *koicha* and *usucha* may be served.

—TOSHIKO MORI

Foreword to the 1804 edition

IN ANGLING, *a line with a lure at the end is dropped into the water to catch the fish. Now, in order to allure and entertain a guest, what should be presented by the host? When an important guest is treated so well that he wishes to remain in the house much longer, then the joy of both guest and host is greatest.*

Chikamatsu Shigenori, a vassal of the Owari clan, conceived the idea of writing this book. He collected various anecdotes about people who had distinguished themselves in the society of the tea ceremony. These people range from imperial princes down to hermits withdrawn from the world. Chikamatsu finally compiled these stories in three volumes with illustrations inserted here and there. He called the book Stories from a Tearoom Window, *and it clearly reveals the true pleasures found in the tea ceremony by those interested in it. Gentlemen attending the tea ceremony generally have felt that idle talk or gossip should be avoided, but*

FOREWORD

Chikamatsu declared that silence is not necessarily a virtue at the tea ceremony. Rather, it is the pleasure of entertaining guests with the utmost hospitality that is indeed beyond description. Chikamatsu's elaborate work should be sincerely appreciated. The essence of the tea ceremony does not lie merely in the satisfaction of the sense of taste, but in the friendly association of strangers, of those of the lower classes with those of the nobility. In the observance of manners in the severe formalities of the tea ceremony, mutal understanding and friendliness are created. Cannot the casting of a fishing line be compared to the entertainment of happy guests?

When this book was completed, I was asked to write a few words; so here I present my own poor remarks.

—Kimura Toshiatsu

茶窓閒話

Part One

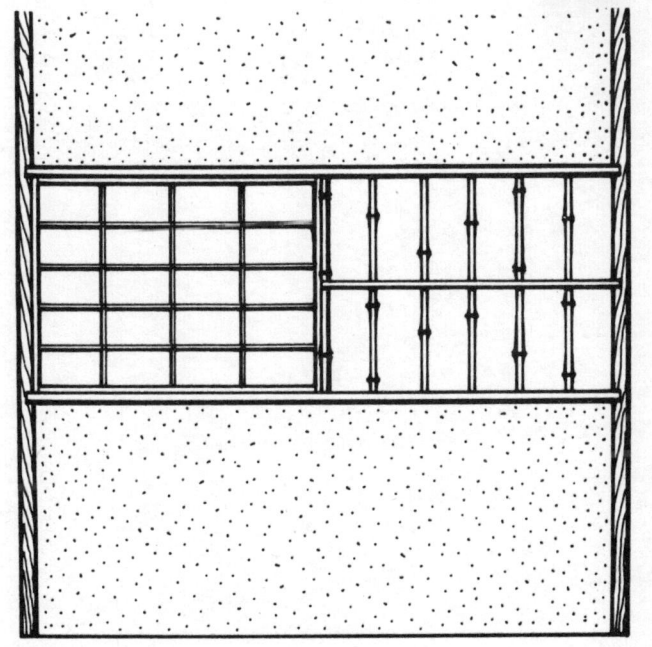

1. Tearooms in the Old Days

In the old days, there were no fixed rules about the dimensions or arrangement of the room used for the tea ceremony. A square hearth was set into the floor wherever it suited the room. For example, a room designed by Murata Shuko is said to have been the size of six *tatami* in area. And the hearth was installed in any of three places, irrespective of the size of room. It is reported that these were the "upper" position, the "lower" position, and a spot quite close to the sill, in front of the utensil *tatami*. Later Takeno Jo-o reduced the size of the room to four and a half *tatami* in area, and the hearth was installed only at about the lower middle of the room. Since then this has come to be called the four-and-a-half-*tatami* style. Afterward, Sen no Rikyu designed a room of three *tatami* and one *daime tatami* in area, and called it the *daimegamae* style. He installed the hearth above the middle of the room. This is the origin of the *daimegamae*-style hearth. The terms "upper" hearth and "lower" hearth, which had long been applied, came to be disused. At present there are very few tea connoisseurs who know of the old style.

*

Murata Shuko (1423–1502): originator of the tea ceremony
tatami: straw floor-mat, about 0.9 by 1.8 meters
Takeno Jo-o (1502–55): tea master and teacher of Sen no Rikyu
Sen no Rikyu (1522–91): the greatest tea master, who perfected the tea ceremony
daimegamae: type of small arbor-style tearoom using *daime tatami* (about three-fourths the size of standard *tatami*)

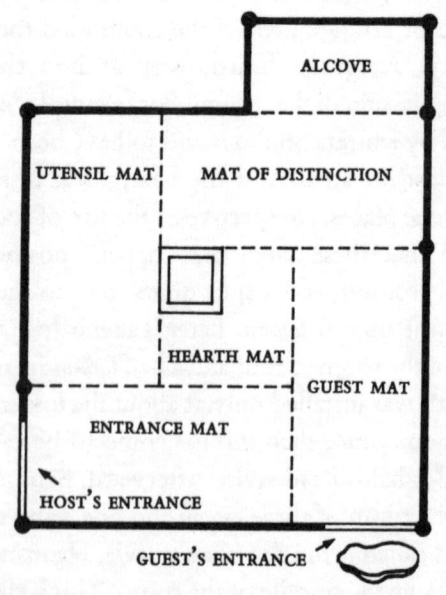

2. Ground plan of a four-and-a-half-tatami tearoom.

2. Lord Yoshimasa's Tearoom

Jishoinden, Lord Yoshimasa, loved the tea ceremony greatly, and Shinno was his instructor. In Lord Yoshimasa's day, the procedures for the tea ceremony were formulated, and its performance was formalized. The lord's room for the tea gathering was eight *tatami* in size, and on the four walls were hung eight scrolls with landscapes by the priest Yujian, including his praise of his own work. Flowers were arranged and displayed as well. It is said that the tea ceremony was held there using a *daisu*.

*

Jishoinden, Lord Yoshimasa: Ashikaga Yoshimasa (1435–90), shogun and supporter of the tea ceremony

Shinno: Nakao Shinno (1397–1471), sometimes called Noami or Shun'osai; tea master, poet, and artist

Yujian: Chinese Zen priest and artist who flourished in the mid-thirteenth century

daisu: tablelike stand used in some types of tea ceremony *(p. 29)*

3. Rikyu's Early Days

Sen no Rikyu was called Yoshiro when young. When he was planning to serve tea for the first time, he asked

Kitamuki Dochin, who was already famous as a venerated tea master in Sakai, to give him instruction. Dochin's friends also joined him in teaching Yoshiro. They all found him to have great qualifications for the tea ceremony and expected him to become an outstanding tea master in the future, but they felt that some correction was needed in his way of serving tea. They said he should not take such large scoops of powdered tea out of the big *chaire* he used. If he would try to use only a small amount of tea and whisk it in a scouring manner, his method would indeed be conspicuously improved. These were their comments. On hearing them Rikyu was able to recognize their true significance, and afterward he developed remarkably, it is said.

*

Kitamuki Dochin: Araki Dochin (1504–62); instructed Rikyu in the tea ceremony and then introduced him to Jo-o

Sakai: trading port near Osaka; birthplace of Rikyu

chaire: ceramic caddy for powdered tea, used in the preparation of *koicha* (thick tea) *(pp. 30, 71)*

4. The Creativity of So-on

Rikyu thought of various innovations. In the tea ceremony using a *daisu*, he reduced the two bags en-

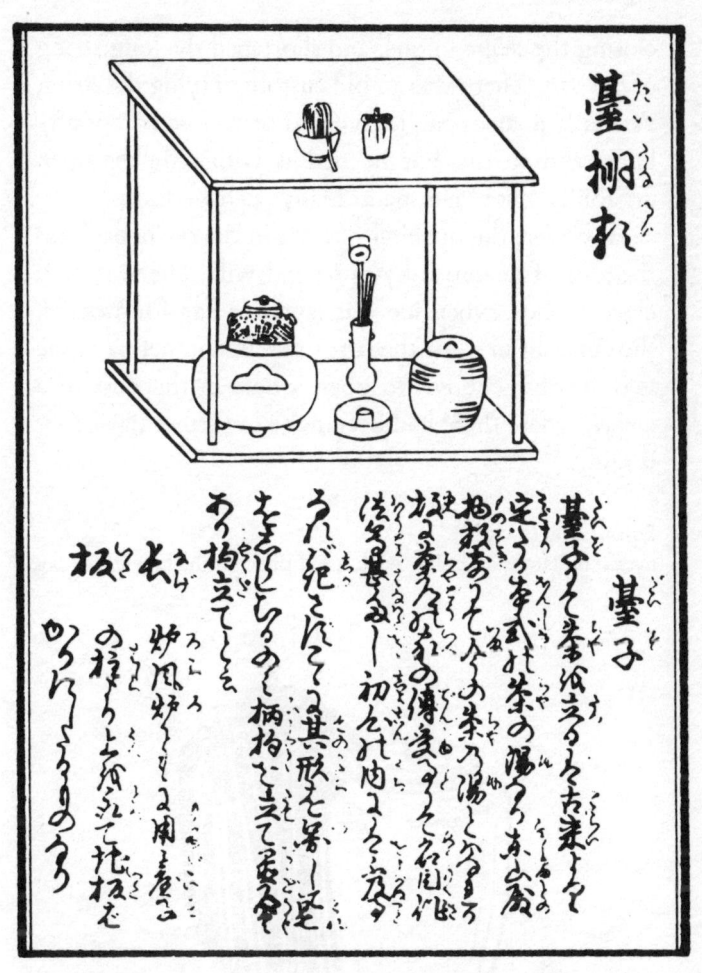

3. Utensils of the tea ceremony arranged on a daisu. *Left to right:* *(above)* whisk in tea bowl, scoop, and tea caddy in cloth bag; *(below)* kettle on brazier, ladle and charcoal chopsticks in ladle stand, kettle-lid stand in waste-water vessel, and fresh-water jar.

closing the *chaire* to one, and shortened the long string of the bag. There was an old custom of tying the string variously in an open dragonfly knot, a closed dragonfly knot, and so on, but he tied it with only the open dragonfly knot. He made many such revisions.

However, the opening of a slit in the *chaire* bag was the idea of So-on, Rikyu's second wife. She was very clever. Once, when she was sewing a bag for a *chaire*, she cut a slit in it for the first time. In another case, she was creative enough to open a hole in the post of a *tankei*, where there had been none in former days, so it is said.

*

So-on: Riki (d. 1600)
tankei: oil lampstand. The wick is fed through the hole in the post.

4. Ceramic tea caddy (katatsuki chaire) and its bag.

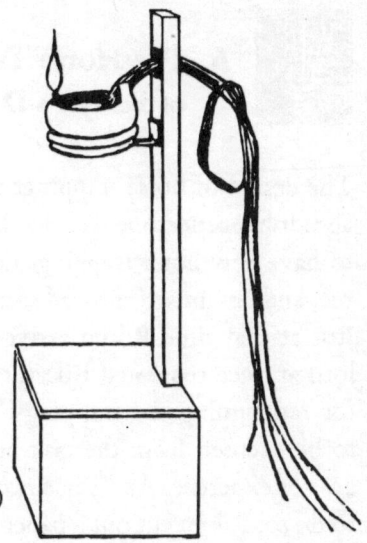

5. An oil lampstand (tankei) used at evening tea.

5. Rikyu the Connoisseur

Rikyu practiced many times distinguishing good *natsume* tea caddies from bad ones among those lacquered by Joami. After much study he was able to make no mistakes even when shown many *natsume* mixed together at random.

*

natsume: lacquered caddy for powdered tea, usually used in the preparation of *usucha* (thin tea); shaped like a *natsume* (jujube) *(p. 58)*
Joami: also known as Joho; considered the finest of lacquerers

[31]

6. The Horse Trappings of Rikyu's Design

The design of horse trappings is not what it was years ago. It happened one day that Lord Nobunaga wanted to have new horse trappings designed for his personal use, and he himself showed some of his ideas for them. Just at that time Rikyu arrived to pay homage. The lord at once requested Rikyu to present his own ideas for redesigning the trappings. At first Rikyu wanted to be excused from the task because it was out of his area of expertise. And yet, since the lord requested him to do so, Rikyu cut out a paper pattern on the spot and presented it to him. Nobunaga accepted it with a compliment, saying, "Well done!" But a while later he said to Rikyu, "That pattern you cut seems to have disappeared, so cut another one." The lord compared the new pattern with the first one and found them not a bit different from each other. He was extremely pleased with this design and decided to adopt it. It has been used ever since. There are many tea utensils known to be of Rikyu's design, but in the case of the horse trappings no recognition of his design was given, probably because he was not after all a warrior.

*

Nobunaga: Oda Nobunaga (1534–82), greatest general of his age and enthusiastic sponsor of the tea ceremony

7. The Ashiya Kettles

茶窓閒話

The Ashiya kettles were cast not at Ashiya in Settsu Province, but at Ashiya in Chikuzen Province. The kettles with designs sketched by Sesshu are said to be the best ones. Sesshu was a man of Iwami Province, but he often traveled to Ashiya and its vicinity. Metal craftsmen at Ashiya asked him to draw sketches for their kettles. It is said that the Ouchi family was most powerful and influential in those days. They employed the metal craftsmen of Ashiya and also invited Sesshu to draw designs which they had cast. His sketches were mostly of pine, cedar, plum, bamboo, and other trees.

Later, in the days of these craftsmen's descendants, it once happened that a criminal who had committed a diabolical crime was sentenced to death by boiling in a caldron cast by Ashiya craftsmen. Since then, tea connoisseurs have disliked newly cast Ashiya kettles. Consequently, the craftsmen were forced to earn their living by casting only kitchen utensils such as pots and pans for daily use.

*

Settsu Province: Hyogo Prefecture at present
Chikuzen Province: Fukuoka Prefecture at present
Sesshu: Sesshu Toyo (1420–1506), Buddhist priest and great
 sumie (ink painting) artist
Iwami Province: Shimane Prefecture at present
Ouchi family: lords of several provinces, including Iwami, and
 patrons of the arts

8. The Temmyo Kettles

The Temmyo kettles were made by the kettle casters of Temmyo in Sano, Kamitsuke Province. They are also called Kanto kettles. The best *meibutsu* kettles were said to be those which were cast at Ashiya or at Temmyo.

*

Kamitsuke Province: Tochigi Prefecture at present
Kanto: district taking in Tokyo and the surrounding area, including Temmyo
meibutsu: article of historical fame

9. Yojiro's Kettles

A man named Tsuji Yojiro lived in Kyoto at the time of Rikyu, and he was a master of kettle casting. His descendants have not followed his art. His kettles are commonly called Kyo kettles. It is said Rikyu loved them so much that he possessed many kettles cast by Yojiro.

*

Kyo: abbreviated form of "Kyoto"

UBAGUCHI

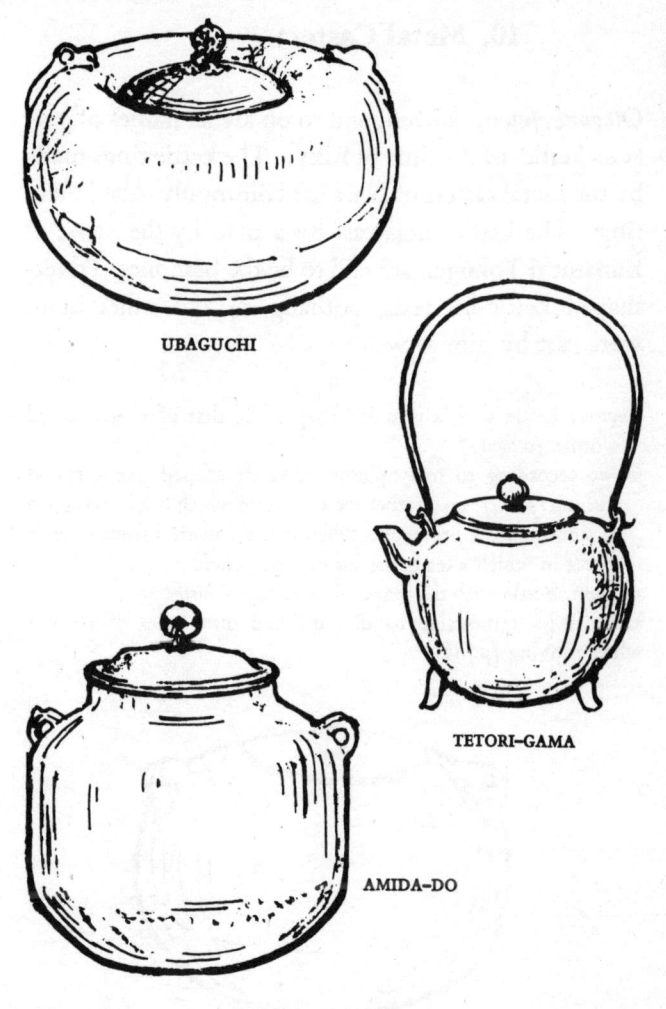

TETORI-GAMA

AMIDA-DO

6. Three kinds of iron kettle.

茶窓閒話

10. Metal Casters

Otogoze, futon, shiribari, and so on are all names of *meibutsu* kettles of the time of Rikyu. The kettle rings made by the metal casters of Nara are commonly called Nara rings. The kettle rings cast by a man by the name of Kanamori Tokugen are said to be the best ones. Trivet-shaped kettle-lid rests, pothangers, and other items were cast by him as well.

*

otogoze: kettle with a rounded shape, like that of a moonfaced woman *(otogoze)*

futon: according to one opinion, a kettle shaped like a round cushion *(futon)*; on another view, a kettle which Rikyu wrapped in a cushion for protection when it was lowered from a castle tower in which a tea gathering had been held

shiribari: kettle with the shape of wide hips *(shiribari)*

kettle rings: removable handles inserted into holes of a kettle when moving *(p. 84)*

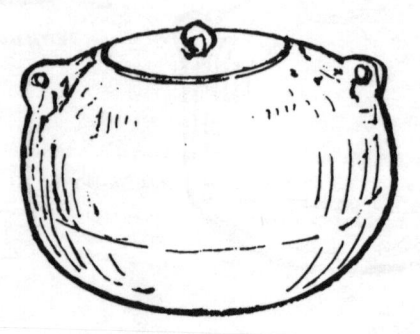

7. Otogoze kettle.

11. The Placement of the Tankei

There seems to be no fixed rule as to where to place the *tankei*. This is said to be a comment made by Rikyu to Lord Nobunaga. *(p. 31)*

12. The Hot Temper of Hideyoshi

While Lord Hideyoshi was pitching camp at Odawara, Rikyu discovered a very fine type of Nirayama bamboo. Rikyu said to the lord that it could be made into an excellent flower container. On hearing this, the lord ordered him to cut the bamboo and work on it. So Rikyu got to work and produced an astonishingly marvelous masterpiece, and presented it to Hideyoshi. Contrary to his expectations the lord did not like it at all, but looked quite displeased with it, and threw it away into the yard. So Rikyu then worked another piece of Nirayama bamboo into a *shakuhachi* flower container, and showed it to Hideyoshi. This time it pleased him very much. Actually the new container was not so good as the first one, Rikyu said to himself, but the lord treasured the new one.

8. Contrary to Rikyu's expectations, Hideyoshi was displeased with

his flower container and hurled it into the yard.

Later, when Hideyoshi put Rikyu to death, the lord was so angry that he broke this flower container and threw it away. Imai Sokyu stealthily picked up the pieces and joined them together, and treasured the container. Years later, Sumiyoshiya Somu of Sakai came to possess it. After his death, Itamiya Sofu bought it at a price of one hundred *kan* and treasured it in his house, so it is said.

*

Hideyoshi: Toyotomi Hideyoshi (1537–98), greatest lord in Japan after Nobunaga's death; learned the tea ceremony from Rikyu
Odawara: city in Kanagawa Prefecture
shakuhachi: lit., "a *shaku* and eight," hence a bamboo flower container 1 *shaku* 8 *sun* (55 cm.) long, with no opening on the side. *(p. 42)*. *Shakuhachi* is also the word for the Japanese bamboo flute.
Imai Sokyu (1520–93): merchant and great tea master
Sumiyoshiya Somu (1534–1603): tea master and disciple of Rikyu
Itamiya Sofu: merchant and tea aficionado
kan: large monetary unit. One *kan* could buy about 20 *koku* (3,608 liters) of rice, i.e., enough to feed an adult for twenty years.

13. The Onjoji Flower Container

The first flower container that Lord Hideyoshi threw away hit a stone in the yard and cracked in some places. Rikyu picked it up and brought it home to Shoan as a souvenir. One day Rikyu hung it above the alcove with flowers arranged in it. His guest noticed that the *tatami* was wet with water leaking from the cracks, and asked Rikyu, "What is the matter with this flower container?"

Rikyu answered, "This leaking of water is very much like human life itself." Rikyu then thought of the sound of the bell of Miidera temple, and wrote "Onjoji, Shoan" on the container. Afterward gold powder was pasted on the writing.

Later this flower container was passed on to Kanaya Sotei, and then Ebara Jisen of Kyoto bought it at a price of eight hundred *ryo*. One day Nomura Soji of Bishu Province, who had been staying in Kyoto, went to his friend Jisen to say goodbye. At that time Jisen said to him, "Do come up to Kyoto again next year without fail, on the occasion of the opening of the tea-leaf jar. The Onjoji flower container, which has not yet been used in a tea gathering, will be on display for the first time." Soji came up to Kyoto again with the sole object of seeing it. The Onjoji really was displayed and the ceremony of opening the tea-leaf jar was conducted. A new tearoom had been constructed, but not a single piece of bamboo was to be seen. This was probably due to Jisen's desire to pay deference to the bamboo of the Onjoji. The tea aficionados of Kyoto admired his taste.

*

Shoan: Sen no Shoan (1546–1614), second son of Rikyu; tea master

Miidera or Onjoji: large temple in Shiga Prefecture, famous for its cracked bell, which Rikyu associates with the cracked flower container

Kanaya Sotei: merchant and tea aficionado

Ebara Jisen (*ca.* 1730): critic of lacquer ware

ryo: monetary unit, equal to about one-fiftieth of a *kan*

Nomura Soji: a very wealthy man

Bishu Province: Aichi Prefecture at present

opening the tea-leaf jar: The new tea leaves harvested in spring are sealed in the jar, which is opened in November or December. Then the leaves are ground into powder, which is kept in the caddy until it is wanted for making tea. *(p. 53, 182)*

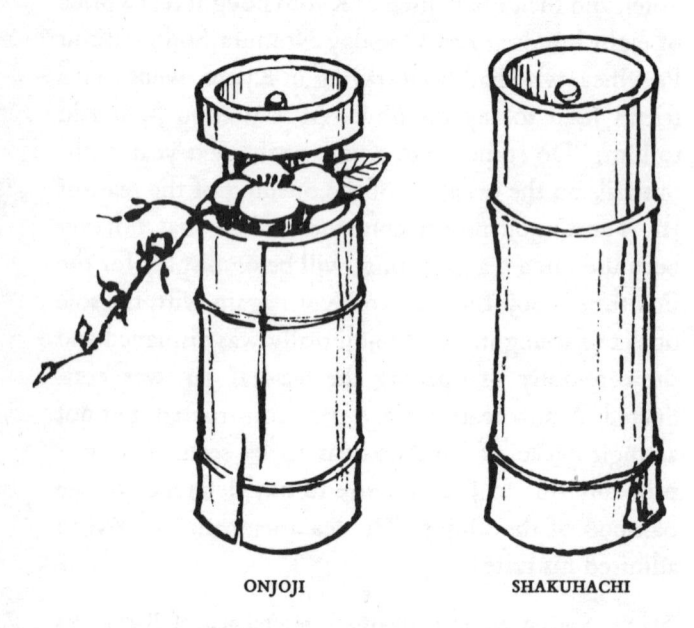

ONJOJI   SHAKUHACHI

9. Bamboo flower-containers.

14. The Value of Onjoji

Ebara Jisen had no children of his own, so he adopted his nephew, Tokusuke, brought him up, and bequeathed all his property to him. Later his family became poor. A merchant of Edo, Fuyuki by name, had desired to obtain the Onjoji flower container. Jisen had purchased it for eight hundred *ryo*, but Jisen's descendants were impoverished, so they asked Fuyuki to buy it for a hundred *ryo* less. Fuyuki said that it would not be good to lower the price, because that might decrease the value of the utensil. Therefore, he had no wish to have the price reduced to seven hundred *ryo*, but would purchase it at the original price of eight hundred *ryo*. It was sold to Fuyuki as he desired.

*

Edo: the old name for Tokyo

15. The Mozuya Katatsuki

The *katatsuki* tea caddy named for Mozuya is a *mei-*

butsu very well known in the world. It is said to have been possessed by Oda Uraku.

*

katatsuki: *chaire* with protruding shoulders *(p. 71)*
Mozuya: Mozuya Soan, Rikyu's son-in-law; tea master of the late sixteenth century
Oda Uraku: Oda Nagamasu (1547–1621), younger brother of Nobunaga; feudal lord and tea master

16. Nampo's Fukusa

The Buddhist priest Nampo was summoned by Retired Emperor Go-Fushimi, so he went up to the palace in the autumn of the third year of the Kagen era (1305). His remarks pleased the retired emperor very much. Nampo then served tea to the retired emperor, who appeared very happy and gave the remainder of the tea to Nampo. Nampo accepted the tea bowl not directly into his hands, but on a *fukusa* which he had with him, and then drank the tea. This is said to be the origin of the use of the *fukusa* in the tea ceremony.

*

Nampo: Nampo Jomyo (1235–1309), great priest who studied in China
Retired Emperor Go-Fushimi: r. 1298–1301
fukusa: silk cloth used to receive the tea bowl, and wipe off utensils in the tea ceremony

17. The Fukusa of Shioze

The best *fukusa* are those made in Kyoto by Shioze, whose ancestors extend back through the Song dynasty in China. He is said to be a descendant of Lin Heging. When the Buddhist priest Ryuzan Zenji II of Kenninji temple returned from Song China, Lin Jinyien, whose art name was Shioze, followed him. Lin Jinyien first lived in Nara, and later moved to Karasumaru street in Kyoto. He had a son while living in Japan, it is said, and he returned alone to Song China, leaving his son here.

*

Song dynasty: 960–1279
Kenninji: first Zen temple in Japan, built in Kyoto in 1202

18. Dochin's Tearoom

The tearoom of Kitamuki Dochin faced west. One day a guest said with apprehension that the setting sun might shine into this room, and asked how that would be. Dochin answered that he always held the tea ceremony in the morning, so he had no time to worry about the good or bad of the beams of the setting sun.

19. Flowers in the Tea Garden

Jo-o taught Rikyu about the garden outside the tearoom with a poem:

> Look with deliberate attention
> At the flowers in the autumn,
> And you will surely find
> Various flowers in the grass.

Can the true significance of this poem be understood? In the olden days flowering trees or plants were not disliked in the garden; but Kobori Enshu did not plant flowering trees in his garden, so that the flowers arranged in his tearoom might be the more appreciated. Since then there has been a rule not to plant flowering trees in the garden.

*

Kobori Enshu: Kobori Masakazu (1579–1647), feudal lord, tea master, poet, architect, etc.

20. Harmony and Contrast

Kanamori Sowa taught a man named Kato that in the tea ceremony what is most important is the re-

10. View of tearoom from the garden, showing the small entrance (kuguriguchi) for the guests.

lationship of harmony and contrast. For example, in the garden of a fine reception room built of plain wood, there may be planted pines, firs, oaks, and so on, and through this vista of a thick growth of trees, a straw-thatched tea arbor can be seen in a recess of the garden. This would show harmonious contrast.

In a rural area, there may be mostly humble straw cottages around, with only one exception: that of a high two-storied house with a massive storehouse adjoining it. It looks high and beautiful in its understated surroundings. Such richness and nobility in the midst of wild simplicity can be called truly attractive. This is nothing other than the harmonious contrast of the tea ceremony.

Now a scroll written by a high priest may be hung in the alcove of a tearoom, and later in the second course of the tea ceremony, fresh flowers may be artistically arranged in a flower container made from a gourd or green bamboo. A *meibutsu chaire* made in ancient China or in the old Seto area may match a newly made bowl of Raku ware or some local ware. This can also be said to present attractive harmony and contrast. But it is not good to try to make things look too interesting, as this is liable to cause them to lose harmony. Nor is it good to use the same arrangement repeatedly. Occasional and seasonal alterations are indeed essential.

*

Kanamori Sowa: Kanamori Shigechika (1584–1656), feudal lord and tea master

Seto: town in Aichi Prefecture known for the production of ceramics

Raku ware: kind of hand-molded earthenware *(p. 149)*

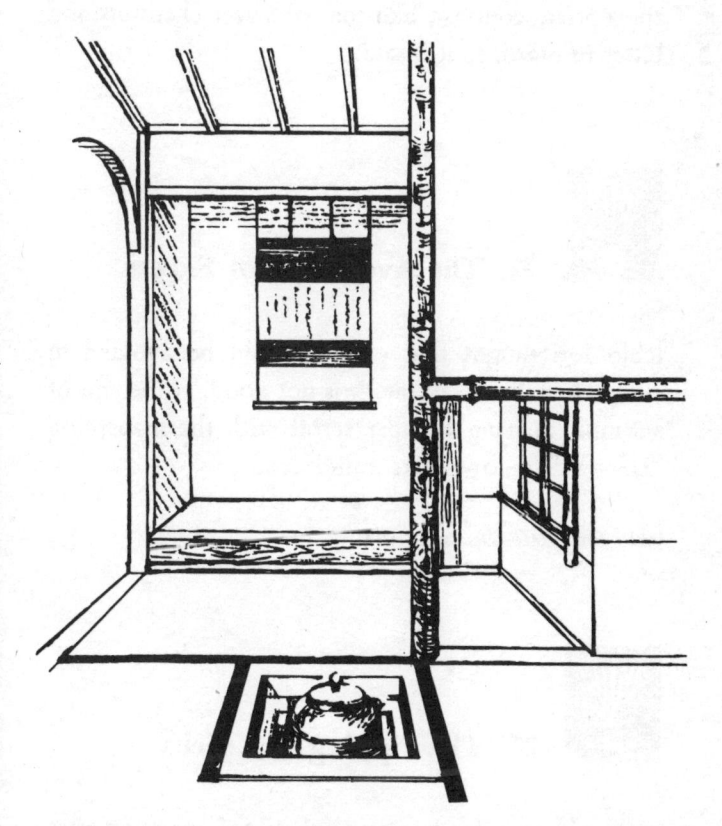

11. Interior of a tearoom, with a kettle on the hearth and a calligraphy scroll hanging in the alcove.

21. Chestnuts and Mustard

Rikyu taught that utensils to be used in the tea ceremony should be cleverly selected so as to attain the appropriate contrast, like that of sweet chestnuts and bitter mustard, so it is said.

22. The Avoidance of Excess

Ichio Iori taught that excess should be avoided in everything. For example, it is not good, at the end of autumn, to hang a paper scroll with the inscription "Leaves fall down like raindrops."

*

Ichio Iori (1602–89): tea master

23. The Sipping of Koicha

In the old days, *koicha* was prepared for one guest after another individually. This usually took such a long time that both the guests and the host became rather bored. Rikyu changed this tedious procedure to the simple one of having the guests all sip tea from the same bowl.

茶窓閒話

*

koicha: lit., "thick tea"; a method of preparing powdered tea for drinking. Rikyu's procedure is now usual.

24. The Sipping of Usucha

There lived in Kyoto a priest named Toyobo, who stayed at Shinnyodo temple. He was very fond of the tea ceremony and became a disciple of Rikyu. He attained the honor of *wabisuki*. He had a scroll inscribed with six Chinese characters adoring Buddha written by Prince Son'en, mounted on paper according to Rikyu's preference. Toyobo possessed only one Ise *temmoku* tea bowl, and he never extinguished the fire in the hearth. One day he invited some close attendants of Lord Hidetsugu to the tea ceremony and served *usucha* to them. As these guests were all busy people with little time to spare, he prepared big servings of *usucha* so that all could sip from the same bowl, instead of using the formal procedure for *usucha*, which would have taken longer. This way of serving tea was quite appropriate for such an occasion. Rikyu praised him and other people spoke well of him, too. To prepare big servings of tea came to be called serving tea in the Toyo manner.

*

Toyobo: Toyobo Chosei (1515–98), priest and tea connoisseur
wabisuki: Rikyu established four ranks for tea connoisseurs: (1) *meijin* (master); (2) *sukisha* (expert); (3) *wabisuki* (moderate expert, possessing no outstanding utensils); (4) *chanoyu-sha* (ordinary tea connoisseur).
Ise *temmoku*: type of *temmoku* tea bowl. According to one view, they were made in Ise Province (Mie Prefecture at present); on another view, one was owned by a man named Ise.
temmoku: type of tea bowl first imported from China, then made in Japan *(p. 99)*
Hidetsugu: Toyotomi Hidetsugu (1568–95), Hideyoshi's nephew
usucha: lit., "thin tea"; a method of preparing powdered tea for drinking, less formal than *koicha*. Toyobo's procedure is not usual.

25. The Homecoming of Naya Suke-emon

In the year Mizunoto-Mi of the Bunroku era (1593), a merchant of Sakai in Izumi Province, Naya Suke-emon by name, went abroad to Luzon and brought back fifty tea-leaf jars. The following year he asked the chief magistrate of the town, Ishida Mokusuke, to present Chinese umbrellas, ten candles, and two live musk deer, together with the tea-leaf jars, to Lord Hideyoshi. The lord looked at the jars, and requested Rikyu to classify them and to set a price on each. He had them all exhibited in the room next to his inner reception room, and put on sale for those who wished to buy them. In four or five days all but three jars were sold. Therefore Suke-emon wanted to take the remaining ones home, but he was told that they had already been taken for purchase by the lord himself. Since then such excellent tea-leaf jars have come to be called *matsubo*.

*

Izumi Province: Osaka Prefecture at present
Luzon: largest island in the Philippines

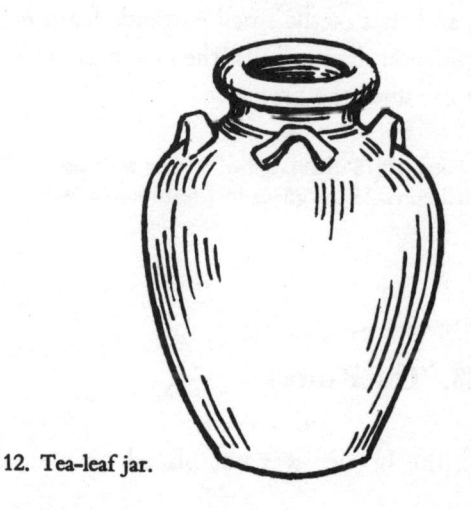

12. Tea-leaf jar.

26. The Position of the Legs

It is said that when Rikyu served tea, he used to squat on two legs, placing his hips firmly on the *tatami*. Doan, on the other hand, is said to have squatted on only one leg.

*

Doan: Sen no Doan (1546–1607), eldest son of Rikyu; tea master

27. Sotan's Terminology

Sotan changed the name of the tearoom from *sukiya* to *kozashiki,* and that of the small entrance from *nijiriguchi* to *kuguriguchi*. It seems that the new names have continued in use until the present.

*

Sotan: Sen no Sotan (1578–1658), son of Shoan; tea master
kuguriguchi: small entrance for guests in a tearoom *(p. 47)*

28. The Koita

At one time, the brazier was not placed on a small

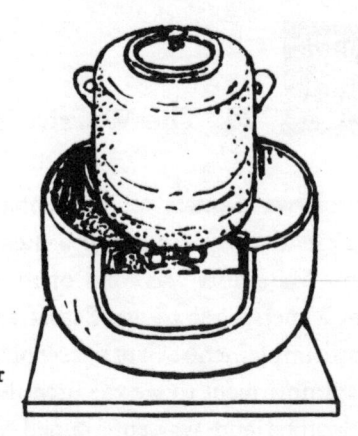

13. Tea kettle and brazier on board (koita).

board. In the age of Jo-o, there lived at Kai street in Sakai a firewood dealer by the name of Sanji. He was a *wabisuki* and was very good at the tea ceremony. For years he was taught by Jo-o how to appreciate the subtle elegance of the tea ceremony. One year, at the ceremony of opening the brazier, he invited his teacher Jo-o to his tearoom. He had polished a large square tile, and placed it in a good position at a corner of the utensil *tatami*. He positioned the brazier on it, put on the kettle, and served tea without any other valuable utensil. Jo-o appreciated it very much. It is said that later a long board was cut into two parts, which were named *koita,* and used for this purpose.

*

opening the brazier: The brazier is generally used in the warm months, and the hearth in the cold months. Usually the brazier is opened and used in May, for the first time in the year.

29. The Warrior's Implements

Hosokawa Sansai, an influential man of his time, possessed many *meibutsu* tea utensils. Hotta Kaga-no-kami Masamori was fond of the tea ceremony, so he sent a messenger to ask Sansai to show him his treasured implements. Sansai accepted his request. When Masamori went to see the utensils, he was most kindly welcomed and was entertained with the utmost hospitality. Then he was shown quite a number of implements, but quite contrary to his expectations, they were all weapons and armor. Masamori felt unhappy as his expectations had not been satisfied, and yet he left thanking Sansai politely for his hospitality.

A few days later, the messenger returned and rebuked Sansai, saying, "Why didn't you show my master your tea utensils?"

The answer was "I did not show them because, when you first came here, you simply asked me to show your master my treasured implements. When we speak of treasured implements in a warrior's house, the meaning can be nothing but weapons and armor. Therefore I did not exhibit my tea utensils at all."

*

Hosokawa Sansai: Hosokawa Tadaoki (1563–1645), feudal lord and disciple of Rikyu. Here he implies that warriors should remember their military vocation, and avoid overindulgence in the tea ceremony.

Hotta Kaga-no-kami Masamori (1608–51): feudal lord

30. The Origins of Tea

During the Konin era (810–24), Emperor Saga ordered the compilation of the anthology called *Bunka Shureishu*. In this anthology, there is a poem composed by Nishikoribe no Hikogimi on the subject of "The Rural Temple of the Priest Nikko":

> Talking with one another,
> Enjoying a bowl of green tea.
> Flowers shrouded in mist
> Bloom amidst the clouds.

This poem shows that tea was enjoyed in our country in ancient times. The priest Myoe is said to have grown tea plants at Togano-o. Probably he had been given some tea seeds from China, and planted them there. He taught people how to make tea.

*

Emperor Saga: r. 809–23; good calligrapher, fond of literature
Nishikoribe no Hikogimi: nobleman serving the emperor
Myoe: Koben Myoe (d. 1232), priest and scholar who built a temple at Togano-o
Togano-o: on the outskirts of Kyoto

31. The Oshiroidoki Natsume

Oshiroidoki are a kind of *natsume* tea caddy. They were first used by Rikyu and are still being used now. Miyake Daichin records that Rikyu treasured his *oshiroidoki*, and it is still preserved in Kyoto. A picture of falling plum blossoms is said to be drawn on its case. The favorite *oshiroidoki* of Sotan is said to have been of a larger size.

*

oshiroidoki: originally cosmetics cases, later used as *natsume*

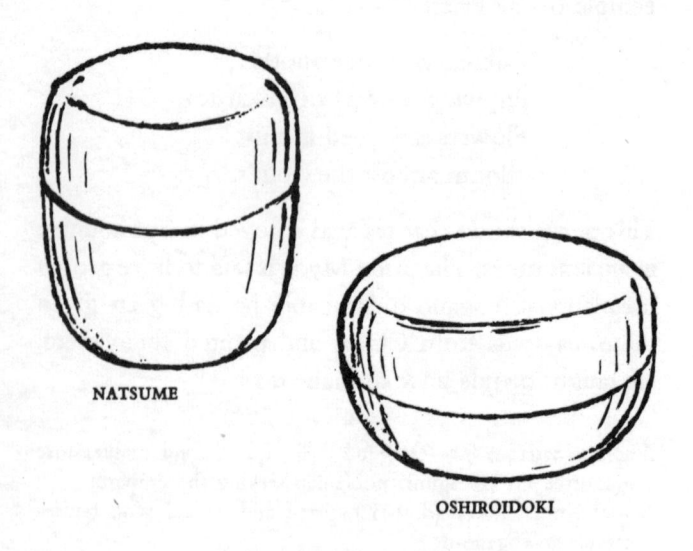

NATSUME

OSHIROIDOKI

14. Lacquer tea caddies.

32. The Size of the Hearth

Before the time of Jo-o, the size of the hearth was 1 *shaku* 5 *sun* 7 *bu* (48 cm.) square. But Jo-o thought this was a little too large and not good construction, so he shortened it for the first time to 1 *shaku* 4 *sun* (42 cm.) square. It is said that this smaller size has been used since then.

33. The Kind Attention of a Guest

Sansai and Rikyu went together to the house of Sumiyoshiya Somu to attend a tea gathering there. When the two guests were about to enter the tearoom initially, the host appeared to greet them and said, "Just now the water for tea was brought in unexpectedly." Then he took the kettle and retired into the kitchen. During the host's absence, Rikyu took the charcoal container from the shelf and arranged the charcoal. Then Somu reappeared with the full kettle in his hand. He saw and appreciated the well-arranged charcoal, gave proper greetings, and put on the kettle. Sansai often told this story and said, "The manners of both the host and the guest remain quite impressive and

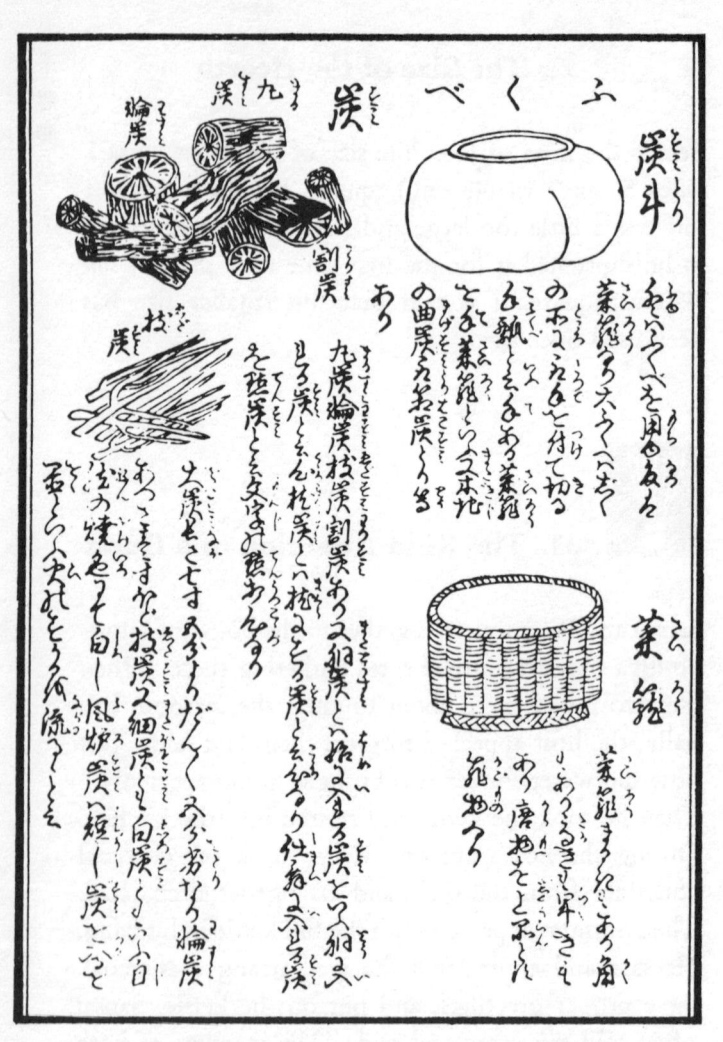

15. Charcoal and charcoal containers. Gourd container *(above, right)* is for winter use and the basket container *(below)* for summer.

vivid in my mind." In those days the so-called *meisui* was the water of Samegai, Yanagi-no-mizu, Ujibashi Sannoma, Sumiyoshi Tengachaya, and so on.

*

meisui: good water suitable for making tea
Samegai, etc.: springs and wells selected by Hideyoshi for *meisui*

34. Dohachi's Scroll

Oda Saemon Yorinaga Nyudo Unjoji, who was called Dohachi after his retirement, possessed a great many *meibutsu*. Among his treasures was a picture of Bodhidharma done by Yan Hui. While Dohachi was living in his hermitage at Maruyama in Kyoto, he wrote his self-praise on this paper:

> It may seem a little deficient
> That this might be my own thought:
> Bodhidharma in ancient days
> Is at present Dohachi himself.

This scroll is said to be owned by Maruyama Shoami now.

*

Oda Saemon Yorinaga Nyudo Unjoji (1582–1620): son of Oda Uraku
Bodhidharma: great Indian Zen priest (see also p. 118)
Yan Hui (*ca.* 1300): Chinese artist

35. The Preparation of Charcoal

Until the days of Jo-o it was the usual practice to place the Ikeda charcoal in the hearth without preparation, and then ignite it. After that the kettle was to be placed above it. But Rikyu found that Ikeda charcoal did not burn well, and could look unpleasant in the hearth, when it was first lighted. Therefore, Rikyu ignited the Ikeda charcoal thoroughly beforehand, so that its outer bark was burned white. He then extinguished the fire so that it could be reignited in a shorter time with more ease. He called this the twice-ignited charcoal, and he employed it just before the guest entered.

*

Ikeda: town in Hyogo Prefecture which was famous for charcoal

36. Ukon's Flaw

Lord Uraku once met and talked with some people. He said, "There is a serious flaw in Takayama Ukon's performance of the tea ceremony. Indeed he has good manners, and his ideas are good, too. But he is too squeamish and fastidious to know what it is to be truly clean. Not only the remotest corners of the garden, but also the farthest underside of the veranda is most minutely swept clean, to no end. To hear of this kind of excessive attention to detail seems only stifling. Can't it be said that true harmony is not to be fully realized unless the proper amount of cleaning to be done is well understood? And yet not a few persons like Takayama are found in the world." Not only those who were present, but others also who heard this story agreed that it was so.

*

Takayama Ukon: Takayama Shigetomo (1553–1615), feudal lord and disciple of Rikyu

37. Sweeping the Garden

One day Sotan invited a guest, and so he went out to see to the sweeping of the garden. He ordered that one spider web in a certain corner not be swept away, but left as it was.

16. Sotan supervised the sweeping of his garden.

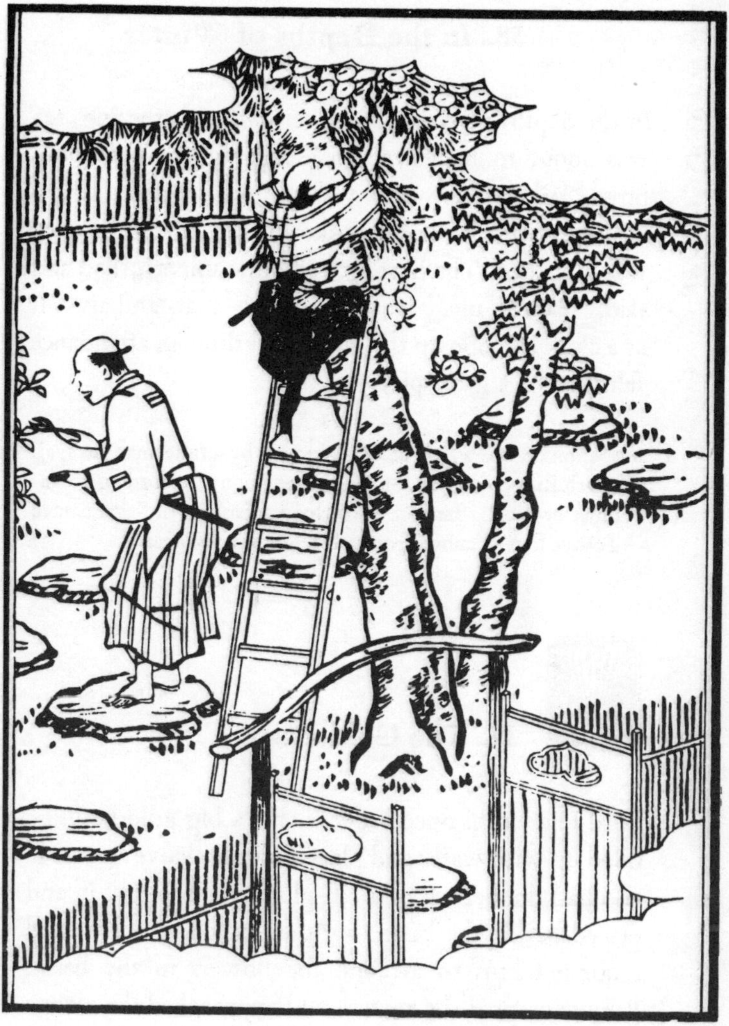

38. In the Depths of Winter

In the depths of winter, at a certain tea gathering, tea was about to be served in a slightly cracked *totoya* bowl. When the water was poured in and the tea whisk rinsed, the bowl broke in two, and the *tatami* was drenched. The host looked quite unperturbed and said, "Excuse me." He took off his coat, and used it as a cloth to wipe up the water. All those in attendance felt it to be a great pity.

*

totoya: on one view, a type of bowl used by a fisherman *(totoya)*, which Rikyu adopted for the tea ceremony; according to another opinion, a kind of bowl that a merchant of Sakai named Totoya first obtained from a foreign ship; Korean

39. The Gold Basin

Lord Hideyoshi once ordered that a big gold basin be filled up with water and placed on the alcove floor. He also had the branch of a red plum tree brought in and placed beside the basin. He then called in Rikyu and requested him to arrange the flowers in the basin. Rikyu accepted the request and approached the alcove quietly. Holding up the plum branch in one hand, he gently stripped the flowers off the branch and into the basin. Then he retired to his seat, carrying the bare branch in his hand. The flowers, some already in bloom, some still buds, mingled together and floated easily on the surface of the water, reflecting the golden brilliance of the basin. It looked wonderfully interesting. Hideyoshi had intended to trick Rikyu, but Rikyu was able to resolve the difficulty skillfully, much to the lord's admiration. In later years, the practice of setting bindweed flowers afloat on the water of a basin became popular. Probably it came from the idea in this legend.

40. The Return of Tanemura to the Capital

In the third month of the third year of the Meireki era (1657), there was a great fire in Edo. During the fire Kano Tan'yu, a painter, handed his treasured *chaire* called Tanemura to a trusted servant, and asked him to run away from the fire in order to save this tea caddy. However, the servant was burned to death on the way, and the box with the tea caddy inside was left beside his burned body. An express messenger who had come down from Kyoto happened to pass by, find the box,

[67]

and pick it up. Judging from the appearance of the box and its bag, this looked to him like something of great value. He took it back to Kyoto and sold the tea caddy to a dealer in imported goods. A man whose name was Tachibanaya Sogen bought it. Those who were shown it said that this was surely an object of great value, perhaps a utensil which by some accident had been removed from a lord's house, and that it might cause trouble in the future. So Sogen notified the authorities about it.

The chief magistrate of Kyoto, Makino Sado-no-kami Chikashige, was also a tea master and a good judge of tea utensils. At his order, the tea caddy was brought in by Sogen. As soon as he saw it, he identified it as the one called Tanemura. He had once been present at a tea gathering held at Tan'yu's house, where Tan'yu had displayed this Tanemura as his treasured utensil. On that occasion, Tan'yu said he had obtained the tea caddy through an agent in Kyoto. Therefore, all the city was searched for that agent. Munesada on Ichijo street was the man who had acted as agent in the handling of this utensil. He said he had written down the size and shape of the tea caddy and kept that record with him. When the caddy was shown him, he recognized it on the spot as the real Tanemura. When the original price was asked, he answered that he had bought it for three hundred silver *kan*.

In the meantime, the details of the discovery were

reported to Tan'yu. He was very glad to hear about it, and at once sent his disciple as a messenger to Kyoto with the necessary amount of money. With the help and efforts of Lord Makino, the tea caddy was safely returned to Tan'yu. The lord gave it the name *miyako kaeri*.

Later, when Lord Makino went down to Edo, Tan'yu came to see him. Thanking him most deeply, he said to the lord, "In return for your kindness, I will paint any pictures you desire."

Makino said, "Then please paint a series of ten views of Mount Fuji for me."

Tan'yu excused himself, saying, "I have never heard of a precedent for this, so I am not sure that I could ever do ten such pictures."

Makino said, "That may well be. My request is perhaps a little too extravagant. You must not have yet attained a full mastery of art, it seems. Any master artist in ancient days could have done such work."

Tan'yu heard this and meditated for a while with his eyes closed, and then he said, "I feel very sorry at my inability to satisfy your request, so I will devote my utmost efforts to doing what you ask. Please tell me the size and scale of the pictures you want." Being told the general outline, Tan'yu began to paint on the very next day, and at last completed the whole series of ten pictures. He presented the pictures to the lord, and they all proved to be exquisite masterpieces. They are now said to be most honorably treasured in the Makino family.

*

Kano Tan'yu (1602–74): painter of the Kano school
Tachibanaya Sogen: merchant
Makino Sado-no-kami Chikashige (1607–77): feudal lord
Munesada: tea connoisseur or curio dealer
miyako kaeri: lit., "return to the capital"

41. The Nakayama Chaire

Tsuda Koheiji, a vassal of Takikawa Sakon Shogen Kazumasu, was a brilliant warrior who distinguished himself in battle as the captain of the vanguard. Afterward, he retired from active service, and changed his name to Koan. He had treasured at home three articles for the purpose of enjoying himself in his old age: his Nakayama *chaire,* Ki Miidera tea bowl, and Kuroki scroll.

Among these three treasures, the Nakayama tea caddy had previously been owned and loved by Hosokawa Yusai. For some reason it came into the possession of Koan, who now lived in Kyoto enjoying the tea ceremony. One day, Koan invited Lord Yusai's son, Lord Sansai, who had long been missing the Nakayama very much and wanting to get it back

[70]

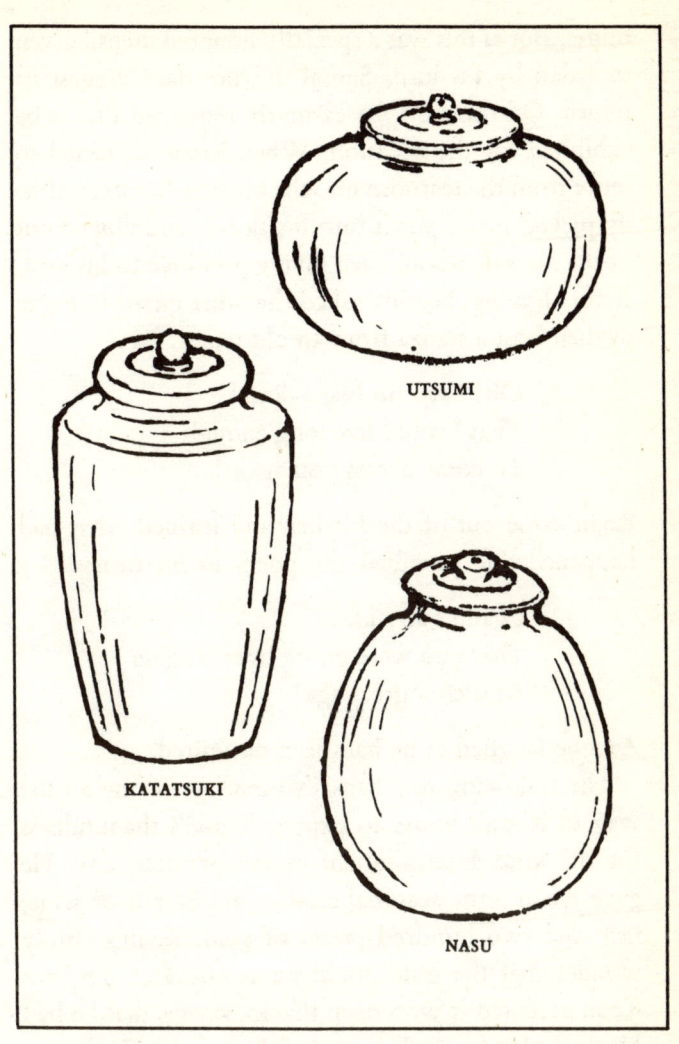

17. Three types of ceramic tea caddies (chaire).

home. But as this was a specially honored utensil given to Koan by his lord, Sansai did not dare suggest its return. On this visit, he earnestly requested that it be exhibited for the occasion. When Koan happened to retire from the tearoom into the kitchen, Sansai stealthily picked it up, put it into his sleeve, and slipped out of the house without even saying goodbye to his host. Before leaving, he only asked the other guests to recite to their host a stanza from an old poem:

> Oh! Sayo no Nakayama!
> That I could live long enough
> To come across you again!

Koan came out of the kitchen and learned what had happened. He parodied the poem in his turn:

> I hadn't any idea
> That you were going over it again
> At such a great age!

And he laughed as he had been outwitted.

The following day Sansai's messenger came all the way to Koan's house to express Sansai's thankfulness for the kind entertainment of the previous day. He gave Koan some seasonal clothes and barrels of wine, fish, and two hundred pieces of gold. Koan's family wondered if the gold could be accepted or not, but Koan accepted it with deep thanks, saying that he had his own plan for making use of the money. With it he built a temple at Kitano as the family temple for his ancestors.

As to the Kuroki scroll, it had been handed down through Koan's descendants to Tsuda Heizaemon, when a certain lord heard of the scroll and wanted to obtain it. The lord asked Lord Enshu to help him by acting as his agent. At last the lord was able to obtain it, and it is said to be treasured in that lord's house.

It was said, "It is all right for Koan to receive the gold coins. But it is not only against the way of *fuga*, but also foolish of him to build a personal temple to pray for the salvation of the departed souls of his own family members. He should have come up with another idea for making use of that money. Those who depend solely on Buddha are not only foolish but incorrect in their way of thinking. Those whose way of thinking is incorrect are liable to be selfish, and are unable to enjoy life together with others. Those who cannot enjoy life with other people cannot enjoy *fuga* at all. There are so many multitudes of the ignorant like Koan in the world now, and very few who really appreciate true *fuga*. Alas!"

*

Takikawa Sakon Shogen Kazumasu (1525–86): feudal lord and disciple of Rikyu

Ki Miidera: famous temple in Wakayama Prefecture

Hosokawa Yusai: Hosokawa Fujitaka (1534–1610), father of Hosokawa Sansai; feudal lord, poet, tea aficionado

Sayo no Nakayama: mountain pass in Shizuoka Prefecture, often mentioned in poems such as this one by the twelfth-century priest Saigyo. The Nakayama *chaire* got its name from this incident.

Kitano: area in Kyoto
fuga: elegant refinement

42. Lord Enshu's Instructions

A certain most honorable lord loved the tea ceremony, and sent his retainer Okabe Doka to Fushimi for three years, in order to learn the tea ceremony from Lord Enshu. This Doka lived to be ninety-seven years old. He lived in the castle town of Daishoji in Kaga Province. He used to say as follows: "Lord Enshu always gave us the following advice about the manners to be observed in the tea ceremony. The preparation of the charcoal, the arrangement of the flowers, the careful handling of the utensils, even to those which the guests have requested to see—the *chaire*, tea scoop, bag, and so on—should all be harmoniously done. It is worst to allow things to look as if they had been placed haphazardly. This was Lord Enshu's repeated advice."

*

Fushimi: area in Kyoto
Kaga Province: Ishikawa Prefecture at present

18. Arrangement of utensils in the kitchen of a tearoom.

43. The Ubaguchi Kettle

There was an *ubaguchi* kettle which was most dearly treasured by Lord Nobunaga. When Shibata Shurinosuke Katsuie was granted Echizen Province, he went up to Azuchi to express his thanks to Nobunaga. The lord showed his loving generosity by himself serving tea for Katsuie, with a word of appreciation for his brilliant military accomplishments. Katsuie took this favorable opportunity to ask for this *ubaguchi* kettle. He said, "If my lord would be so kind as to bestow on me the *ubaguchi* kettle, my happy memories in my old age would be beyond description."

Nobunaga entered another room and after a while returned with the kettle in his hand. He gave it to Katsuie immediately while murmuring a poem to himself:

> You *ubaguchi*, my dearest,
> Never did I tire of sipping
> From you so many, many times.
> You will be sipped from by another—
> Oh! How much will I miss you!

Once previously Katsuie had begged Nobunaga for this kettle. At that time the lord promised to give it to him when he performed a brilliant military exploit in war. Nobunaga remembered his promise when Katsuie successfully conquered Kaga Province.

*

ubaguchi: lit., "hag's mouth," hence a kettle suggesting such a shape (p. 35)
Shibata Shurinosuke Katsuie (1522–83): feudal lord
Echizen Province: Ishikawa Prefecture at present
Azuchi: town in Shiga Prefecture where Nobunaga built a castle

44. The Manners of the Tea Ceremony

Kuze Doku Raisai spoke as follows: "The manners of the tea ceremony originally arose from the serene tastefulness of leisured and retired people, and its embodiment in quiet vacancy and deliberate simplicity. The ceremony or party can be called *suki*. This was originally seen to have nothing to do with worldly wealth or the nobility. However, since Lord Yoshimasa indulged himself in the tea ceremony, it gradually grew into luxurious extravagance. A single earthen vessel came to be more esteemed than a jewel as large as 1 *shaku* (30 cm.) in diameter, and a single scroll came to be more precious than a thousand gold coins. This can be called the current evil of the tea ceremony.

"And yet, the very essence of tea manners is still strictly observed. In attending the tea ceremony, both the host and his guests help each other, bathe and purify themselves beforehand, change clothes, renew their attitude no matter how used to it they are, remain modest and reticent in speech and action, feel as if they were fully satisfied even with nothing, and act as if someone were present even when entering an empty room. Can't this be called respectfulness? One always arrives ahead of the appointed time. If one is late, one must come and apologize for one's lateness. Intercession, daily life, acts and attitudes—all are faithful to the rules and in harmony with the way of righteousness. Can't this be called true courteousness? However wealthy one may be, no beautiful pictures are to be displayed nor gems shown in one's room. As to meals, fewer than three or four kinds of fish or vegetables should be enough even for kings or nobles. Can't this be called true frugality? And yet, harmony is attained in such an environment. Everything is like this in general outline. Isn't it worth observing? The evils that should be complained of lie in the minutest details. Tea aficionados should try to return to the fundamental essentials of the tea ceremony."

*

Kuze Doku Raisai (1704–84): tea master
suki: aesthetic taste

45. Doan's Alcove

The room of four and a half *tatami* which Jo-o used had an alcove of 1 *ken* (1.8 meters) in size. Doan reduced the alcove to 4 *shaku* 3 *sun* (1.3 meters). Rikyu saw this and found it to be much better, so when he had a new room of four and a half *tatami* built, he made an alcove of 4 *shaku* 3 *sun*. Since then many have followed this example.

46. The Hiragumo Kettle

Matsunaga Danjo Hisahide rebelled against Lord Nobunaga and shut himself up in Shigi Castle in Yamato Province, but he was attacked and defeated by Lord Nobutada. As the castle was at last about to fall, Hisahide climbed up the highest tower and threw down the *hiragumo* kettle which he had long loved and treasured, breaking it to pieces. After that he set fire to himself and committed suicide.

This kettle had the design of a flat spider on its surface. As the water in the kettle gradually came to a boil, the spider could be seen crawling about. It was indeed a *meibutsu* well known to the world. Hisahide knew that Nobunaga had long wanted to possess that kettle, so he must have felt jealous at the thought of its being delivered into the hands of his enemy after his death.

*

Matsunaga Danjo Hisahide (1510–77): lord in charge of purging corrupt officials, and of public morals
Yamato Province: Nara Prefecture at present
Nobutada: Oda Nobutada (1557–82), eldest son of Nobunaga
hiragumo: lit., "flat spider"

47. The Fall of Sakamoto Castle

Among the articles and utensils possessed by Lord Nobunaga, his *narashiba katatsuki*, *otogoze* kettle, *efugo* fresh-water vessel, scroll with the calligraphy of Xi-tang, and so on were the *meibutsu*. When Akechi Hyuga-no-kami Mitsuhide rebelled against Nobunaga and attacked Azuchi Castle, these treasures—together with a long sword made by Fudo Kuniyuki, a sword by Niji Kunitoshi, a short sword by Yagen Toshiro, and others—were all carried away to Sakamoto Castle by Mitsuhide's kinsman Akechi Samanosuke Mitsutoshi. But Mitsutoshi's defense of Sakamoto Castle was destined to end that day. So Mitsutoshi urged Mitsuhide's wife and children to go up to the highest tower and prepare some dry grass. Then all the above-mentioned articles and utensils were packed in silk bedclothes and bound tightly with long women's sashes, and the package was carried up to the veranda of the tower.

Mitsutoshi called out in his loudest voice, so that the attacking army might be silenced and listen to what he was going to say. He shouted, "Now I will speak to you. My master, Akechi Hyuga-no-kami Mitsuhide, found no favor with fate, so that he was defeated and died. So now I myself, Akechi Samanosuke Mitsutoshi, am going to kill myself after putting my master's wife and children to death. However, I feel that even as we perish, we will not be able to bear seeing these most valuable articles and utensils ruined with us. Please take these treasures to your commander together with a list of them." So shouting, he lowered the package slowly and carefully down by means of the sashes. The attacking soldiers received it safely and took it to their headquarters. Mitsutoshi watched this with his own eyes, and then went in to stab Mitsuhide's wife and children to death, and set fire to the dry grass. When the tower was half-burned, he cut his belly crosswise, and was burned to death. The thousands of attacking warriors admired him tearfully, finding him to be a truly excellent warrior.

When he is compared with Matsunaga, who broke the *hiragumo* kettle to pieces, what a great difference there is between the two! Indeed, Mitsutoshi can be called the most excellent of warriors.

*

narashiba: *katatsuki* of *nara* (Japanese oak) wood
efugo: fresh-water vessel shaped like an *efugo* (falconry basket)
Xitang (1185–1269): great Chinese priest and calligrapher
Akechi Hyuga-no-kami Mitsuhide (1528–82): feudal lord who, after rebelling against and killing Nobunaga, was soon defeated by Hideyoshi and killed
Sakamoto Castle: in Shiga Prefecture
Akechi Samanosuke Mitsutoshi (1537–82): warrior, tea connoisseur, and cousin of Akechi Mitsuhide, who joined in the attack on Nobunaga and was then besieged in Sakamoto Castle by an ally of Hideyoshi

19. Efugo-shaped fresh-water vessel.

48. The Overlapping of Paper

Rikyu said that the overlapping of the paper strips on a *shoji* frame should be as follows: 1 *bu* (3 mm.) is too narrow, while 1½ *bu* (4.5 mm.) is a little too wide.

*

shoji: papered sliding door

49. Tea Flowers for Rikyu

Rikyu said that it was not advisable to use lycoris or cockscomb in flower arrangements. Even though he did not like flowers of red color or tree peonies, he liked the light color of rose mallows and purple tree peonies, so he arranged them. Herbacious peonies are good when their leaves are attached, but tree peonies are good only when they have no leaves. Loosestrife leaves were often arranged by Rikyu, who found them rather interesting. Some tea masters liked to arrange purple magnolias. They were called *mokuren* or *shigyokuran*, and were rather rare in the past. They were seen growing in front of Toyokuni cemetery, and many people wanted to arrange them in season.

*

Toyokuni (Hokoku): shrine in Kyoto where Hideyoshi's tomb is located

50. Rikyu Taught by a Disciple

A flower container made of basketwork should not be drenched with water. In the old days, such a flower container was placed on a thin board. One of Rikyu's principal disciples happened to place it without using a board. Rikyu saw this and said, "It has long been a routine practice to place the flower container on a thin board, though it is not at all attractive. But now we shall follow the example of my disciple." Since then the thin board has not been used.

51. Big Kettle Rings

Big kettle rings are said to have been cast at the suggestion of Sansai. It is wrong to say that they were not used in the Ichio school, because Ichio Iori often used them.

20. Kettle rings.

52. A Family of Scroll Mounters

Joami 浄阿弥 was a descendant of Nakao Soami, a *dobo* of the Ashikaga family. Joami was well versed in the art of scroll mounting, and was also fond of *renga*. Joha 紹巴, his master in *renga*, gave him the first character from his own name, so Joami's name changed to 紹阿弥 Joami. Then he omitted the middle character, 阿 *a,* from his new name, so that finally his name became Jomi. He lived at Bukkoji temple, east of Karasumaru street in Kyoto. Several generations lived in that same house for about three hundred years, as it never burned down. And that same name, Jomi, has been succeeded to until the present. All the Jomis have been engaged in the work of scroll mounting as their family occupation. They have many documents inherited from their ancestors, so they are all experts in this work and well versed in the historical records of the field.

*

Nakao Soami (d. 1525): grandson of Nakao Shinno; outstanding scroll mounter
dobo: retainer of a shogun or nobleman, in charge of the tea ceremony or other entertainments
Ashikaga family: dynasty of shoguns (1333–1573)
renga: linked verse

53. Iori's Tea Scoop

A certain man possesses a letter requesting a powdered-tea scoop made by Ichio Iori. This letter was sent to a nephew of Iori.

*

a powdered-tea scoop made by Ichio Iori: Iori was very skillful at making tea scoops of bamboo, and so the nephew replied that he held them as dear as "my own little fingers." However, he kindly presented the one requested to his correspondent.

54. The Grimaces of Xushi

While Lord Enshu was staying at Fushimi in Kyoto, Kurota Chikuzen-no-kami Nagamasa sent him a message saying, "I am going to drop in at your house on my way back to my hometown, and I would be much obliged if you would be kind enough to serve me a bowl of tea." So Enshu prepared a tea ceremony for him. But unexpectedly Lord Kurota suddenly fell ill at the station of Otsu, and was forced to remain there in order to recuperate. Therefore he sent a messenger to excuse himself from attending the tea ceremony. Enshu was disappointed to hear the news.

Then Kambayashi Chikuan happened to come by

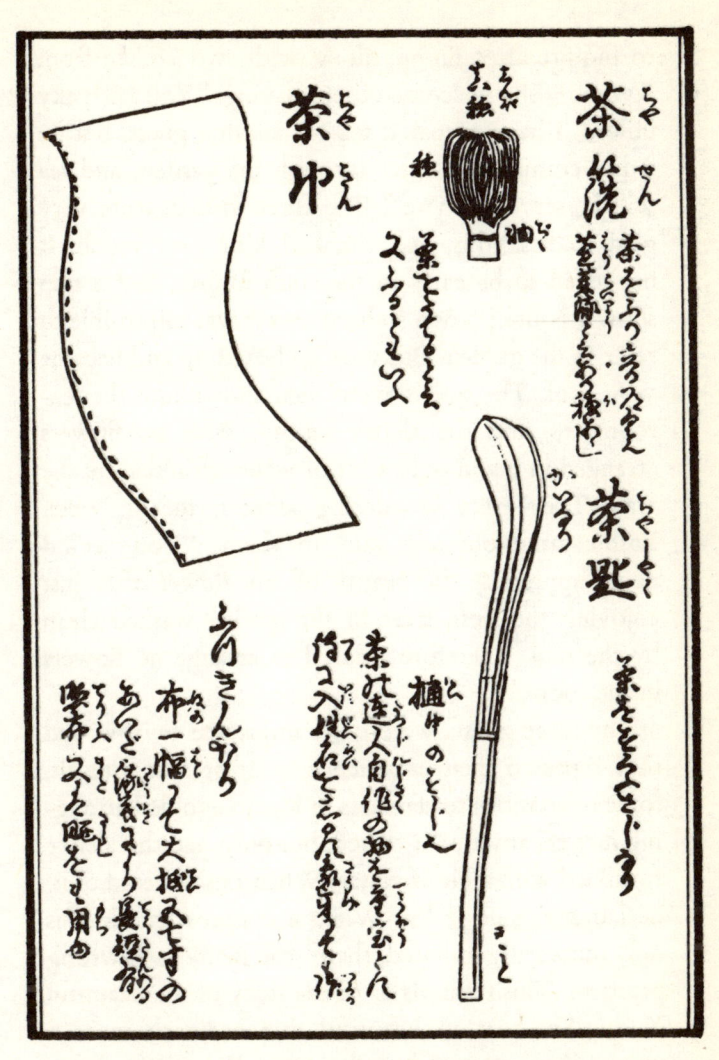

21. Some tea utensils: chakin cloth, tea whisk, and tea scoop.

to inquire after Enshu, along with two *sukisha* from Kyoto. Enshu welcomed them, saying, "You are lucky indeed. I have prepared tea for another guest, but he is not coming. So enter through the garden, and tea will be served to you." The three visitors were very glad to hear this, and thanked him very much. It happened to be early in the sixth month, and a rain shower poured down so hard that it was impossible to relax in the garden. But soon it cleared up and became very cool. The guests were then shown into the tearoom, to find the alcove empty, with no flowers arranged in it and only a bit of water sprinkled on the wall. They were wondering what it meant, when Enshu came out and said to them, "You would never appreciate the beauty of any flower after just enjoying the fresh trees in the garden washed clean by the rain. Therefore I dared to arrange no flowers in the room."

The three guests were quite impressed by this, and they repeated their experience to others. As a result, some dilettantish tea fanciers in Kyoto avoided arranging flowers anytime it rained, but only had the alcove sprinkled with a bit of water. When Enshu heard of it, he laughed quite a bit. When a master's true idea is only outwardly imitated, there arise many such wrong practices. This reminds us of the story of the beautiful Xushi. She was so beautiful that ordinary women imitated everything about her, even her grimaces.

Kurota Chikuzen-no-kami Nagamasa (1568–1623): feudal lord and tea aficionado
Otsu: city in Shiga Prefecture
Kambayashi Chikuan (d. 1600): tea manufacturer
sukisha: expert on the tea ceremony (see p. 52)
Xushi: legendary beauty of China

55. The Essence of Serving Tea

Rikyu's way of serving tea was not elaborate at all. Neither at its start nor at its finish could any conspicuous point of tastefulness be recognized. This can be called the very essence of serving tea, far from simple normality or routine commonness. This was always said by Hariya Soshin.

*

Hariya Soshin: tea connoisseur and disciple of Rikyu

56. Lord Enshu's Way of Serving Tea

Lord Enshu's way of serving tea was not so outstanding nor so tasteful as that of other tea masters at the time, but only smooth and steady. However, after the death of Rikyu, the fame of Enshu was the greatest in the world. This was probably because of his social status.

57. Tea of Sakai, Tea of Kyoto

While Rikyu was alive, the tea ceremony at Kyoto centered mainly on discrimination between good utensils and bad ones. On the other hand, the tea ceremony at Sakai was superior to that of Kyoto. Therefore, Rikyu used a *katatsuki* tea caddy when serving a guest from Kyoto, while he used a *natsume* for a guest from Sakai. It is said that since the end of the Tensho era (1573–92), Sakai has declined and Kyoto has prospered.

58. Kama and Kansu

Kama and *kansu* both have the meaning of "kettle." Both words are so common that many are ignorant of this fact. In the book *Taiheiki,* there is this phrase: "Taking down the nine rings of the pagoda spire, they cast *kansu.*" It is said that there are many people who do not know the meaning of this.

*

Taiheiki: history of fourteenth-century wars, attributed to Kojima Hoshi

59. Flower Arranging

Makino Inaba-no-kami Hideshige arranged flowers for the first course of the tea ceremony using the brazier. One of his close friends asked him about arranging flowers for the first course. Lord Makino answered that in the case of the tea ceremony using the *daisu,* a scroll should be hung and flowers arranged, but there might occur some variations. Flowers brought by the guests, or flowers which might easily fade by the time of a later course, are arranged for the first course. Rikyu arranged morning glories for the first course, and this was considered a good precedent.

*

daisu: (see p. 29)

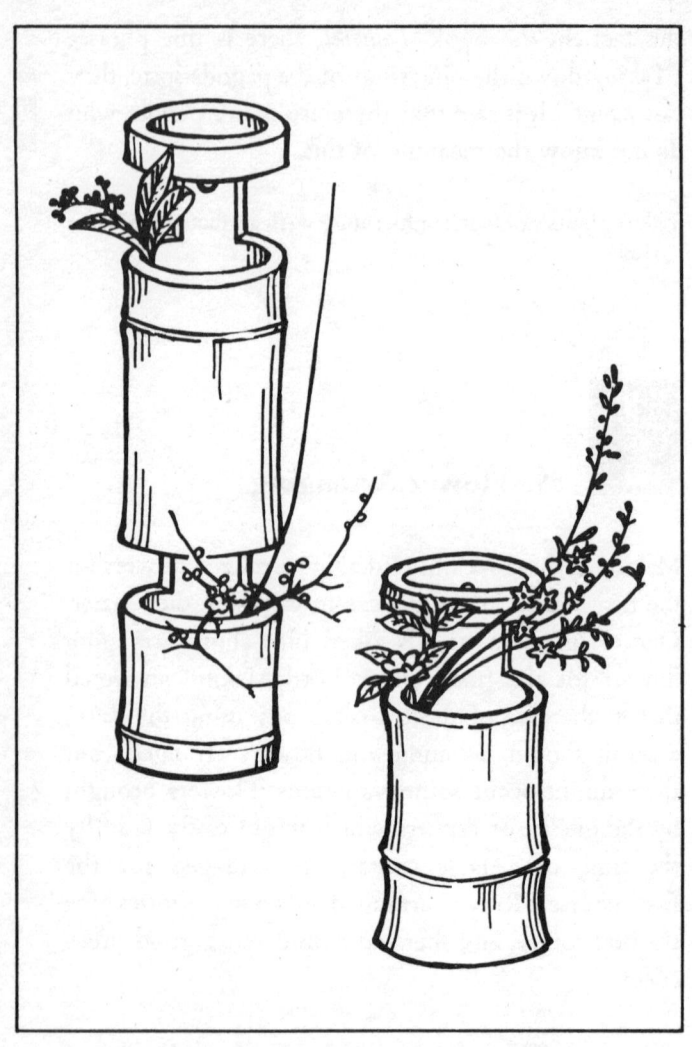

22. Rikyu's flower arrangements in bamboo containers.

60. A Morning Glory and Tea

The legend of Rikyu's morning glory has been passed on with significant import in the old school. One year, Rikyu planted morning glories in his garden. Lord Hideyoshi heard of their brilliant blooming in season, and wanted to see them the next morning. When the lord arrived there, however, not a single morning-glory flower was to be seen in the garden. The lord looked quite displeased. When he entered the tearoom, he found only one morning glory, the most beautiful flower, arranged in the alcove. It looked utterly fresh and glorious. The lord and his attendants felt quite refreshed, as if they had just awakened, and admired it very much. This is commonly known as Rikyu's tea ceremony with a morning glory. It is not certain whether this is a true story or not.

61. Hechikan, Master of Sukido

A man called Hechikan ノ貫 lived in Kyoto, and he was a master of *sukido*. He was also fond of unusual things, and was the best friend of a doctor named Ko Dosan. One day it occurred to Dosan that the Chinese character 貫 *kan* could be replaced by 桓 *kan,* the strokes of which can be rearranged to form 日本一 meaning "number one in Japan." The character ノ *hechi* is half of 人 "man." Therefore, when *hechi* and *kan* are combined into Hechikan, it may mean "Even half a man is number one in Japan."

Hechikan's ideas, though they may sound somewhat extraordinary, were based on a full understanding of Buddhism, so they are not really extraordinary at all. Many of his acts can be used as standards or examples in the present world. The tea-leaf jar had long been placed at the very center of the alcove, but one day Hechikan dared to display it at the *kuguriguchi*. While he was living at Yamashina, he used to cook porridge in one handy pan every morning. He ate from it, and after eating he polished it with sand. He also used it to draw water from a clean river at the foot of a mountain, which he boiled on the hearth to enjoy tea. He composed an amusing poem:

> Oh, you kettle,
> Your mouth is protruding
> A little too much.
> Don't tell the others
> I cooked porridge in you.

Rikyu often heard about Hechikan, and one day he

decided to visit him with some friends. There was a stone well just in front of his house, which faced a busy highway where men and horses were passing by all the time, stirring up mud and dust all around. The visitors thought it would be impossible to drink tea from such water, and they wanted to go back. Hechikan overheard this and stepped from his house, crying out loudly, "The water for tea comes from another source, and yet you are returning?" Rikyu heard this and came back with the others. They had a good talk, as if they had long been close friends, and it is said that afterward their friendship deepened.

*

Hechikan: Sakamotoya, merchant and tea connoisseur
sukido: the way of aesthetic taste, pursuit of the tea ceremony
Ko Dosan: Manase Dosan (1507–94), great doctor
Yamashina: town on the outskirts of Kyoto

62. Fukuami's New Year's Day

At Shimokyo in Kyoto there lived a poor man named Fukuami. From morning till night he enjoyed tea and life.

This was a New Year's Day poem:

The soot is not swept away,
The New Year's decorations are not displayed,
Rice cakes are not pounded,
And yet, even to such a house
Spring never fails to return.

Who composed this poem is not really known. If the writer of this poem should happen to be Fukuami, then his *furyu* would be beyond admiration. Many such wonderful men of taste remain completely unknown, and this is truly to be regretted.

*

Fukuami: tea connoisseur and disciple of Rikyu
furyu: elegant refinement

63. Tea and Zen

The priests of Daitokuji temple insisted that modern tea practices would not be interesting without calligraphy. What is more, they said that even in a small tearoom no calligraphy or paintings should be hung except those done by Zen priests. Such a mundane custom was accepted because tea connoisseurs were generally illiterate, while priests alone were literate and therefore highly respected. All Zen priests were thought to be rather clever and cunning, to have a talent for inducing others to enter the way of Zen, and also to have exhaustively absorbed both the tea ceremony and the philosophy of Zen. It would certainly be wrong to misinterpret the idea of the tea ceremony as being based solely on the essence of Zen, wherein it is said, "Inhaling all the wind in the pine trees, the soul is never soiled." But the calligraphy of Zen priests alone came to be accepted. Shuko, the progenitor of *sukido*, was a disciple of the Zen priest Ikkyu, Jo-o of Daikyu, and Rikyu of Kokei, while Sotan was taught by a disciple of Shun'oku. Lord Enshu, Sakuma, and others were disciples of Kogetsu. Other tea masters, following these examples, went to Zen temples, and displayed on their walls calligraphy by priests whom they revered. Afterward, people who observed their example thought that calligraphy by Zen priests should be used on the occasion of the tea ceremony.

In ancient days, various masterpieces of painting and writing from both China and Japan were often used. Therefore, prejudiced imitation of particular examples should be avoided. Actually, calligraphy by Zen priests is generally unbelievably bad and hardly worthy of appreciation, because they do not study the art very comprehensively. And they often write with an abusive spirit, so that their tempers are reflected in their works, which makes them look quite miserable. And yet, the tasteless and unreal phrases of such calligraphy are often introduced by ignorant people as if they were invaluable maxims. Such people value only money and neglect true insight. They appreciate insignificant rumors and are pleased with anything at random. Can it be proper to value things only because of their price? Someone has said that a clear moon and a fresh wind can be enjoyed without paying any money. Can any object of historical fame equal the appreciation of the fresh air? Those who have true insight should deeply consider this truth, and then the essence of elegance and taste can easily be realized.

*

Daitokuji: Zen temple in Kyoto
Ikkyu: Ikkyu Sojun (1394–1481), Zen priest
Daikyu (1468–1549): Zen priest
Kokei: Kokei Sochin (1532–97), Zen priest
Shun'oku: Shun'oku Shuen (1529–1611), Zen priest
Sakuma: Sakuma Sanekazu (1570–1642), feudal lord and tea master
Kogetsu: Kogetsu Sogan (1574–1643), Zen priest

64. The Chakin

A *wabi* tea connoisseur in the countryside sent one gold *ryo* to Rikyu, asking him to purchase some tea utensils with it. Rikyu bought *chakin* with the money and sent back the change, telling him that tea could be enjoyed as long as the *chakin* was clean, because *wabi* could exist even in the absence of everything else.

茶窓閒話

*

wabi: quiet and simple taste—the ideal of the tea ceremony
chakin: linen cloth used to wipe the rinsed tea bowl *(p. 87)*

65. A New Temmoku Bowl

A tea master said that when tea is served to a nobleman, a new *temmoku* bowl or some other new bowl should be used.

23. Temmoku tea bowl on its stand (temmoku-dai).

[99]

66. The Screen

Jo-o placed a folding screen near the hearth when he used a room larger than four and a half *tatami* in size. This screen was 2 *shaku* 6 *sun* (79 cm.) high, with black blade-edges on both top and bottom. The screen hid the *dai-temmoku* tea bowl so that it could not be seen from the outside. But since the time of Rikyu the height of the *daisu* has been reduced by 1 *sun* 5 *bu* (5 cm.), so it was said that the screen itself should be shortened by as much.

*

dai-temmoku: *temmoku* bowl placed on a stand (*dai*)

67. The Gourd Flower-Container

The idea of a flower container made from a gourd is said to have originated from the gourd carried by a pilgrim. Rikyu saw this pilgrim passing by with a canteen made from a gourd at his waist. Rikyu desired the gourd, and when he obtained it he made a flower container of it. He named it Gankai. Since then people have come to like gourd flower-containers. *(p. 102)*

*

Gankai: the Japanese name of Yan Hui (*ca.* 500 B.C.), scholar and disciple of Confucius

68. Flower Containers of Bamboo

茶窓閒話

A flower container of bamboo is called *hitoyo-giri* when one opening for the flowers is cut in the side, and *futayo-giri (niju-giri)* when there are two openings. Rikyu used one of the latter to hold extra flowers in reserve, and hung it in his kitchen. One day, out of curiosity to see how it would look, he hung it in his small tearoom, and so it is often used in small tearooms now. But this is not an advisable practice.

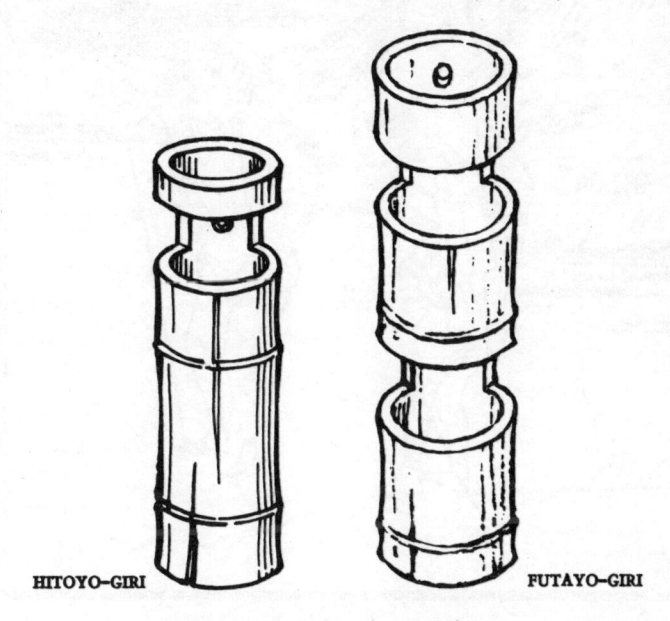

HITOYO-GIRI   FUTAYO-GIRI

24. Bamboo flower-containers.

25. Rikyu saw a pilgrim passing by with a gourd at his waist.

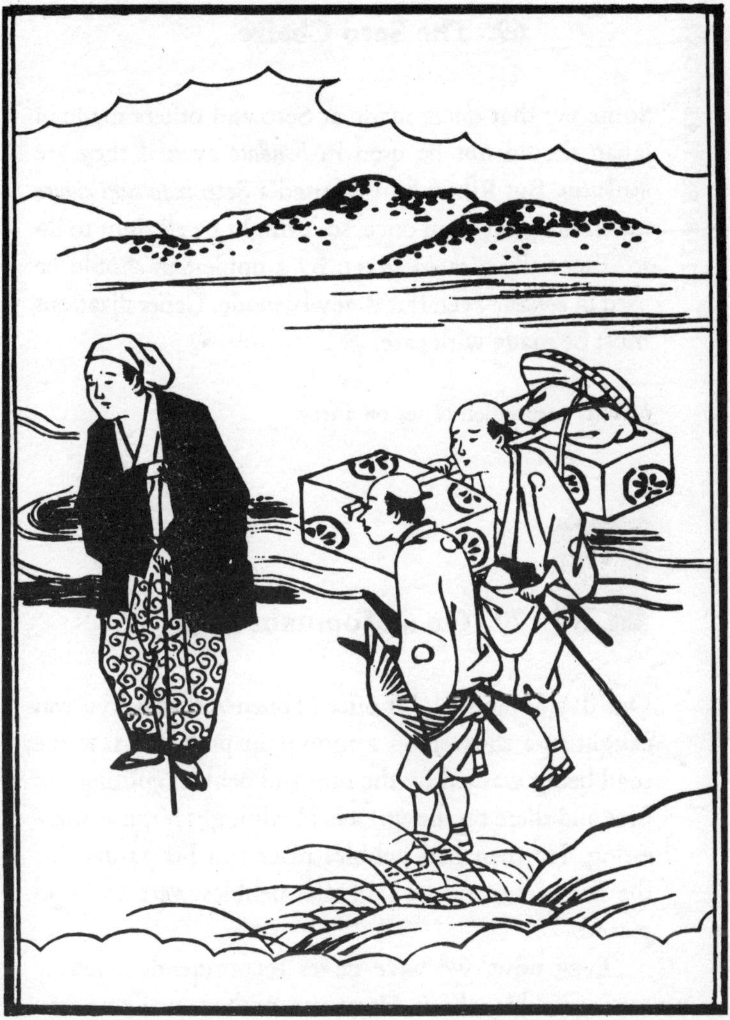

69. The Seto Chaire

Some say that *chaire* made at Seto and others made in Japan should not be used in *bondate* even if they are *meibutsu*. But Rikyu himself used a Seto *katatsuki chaire* in *bondate* more than once, so it might be all right to do so. Especially a *chaire* given by a nobleman should be used in *bondate* even if it is newly made. Generalizations must be made with care.

*

bondate: preparation of tea on a tray

70. On a Mountain Path

One day Sotan said, "It once happened that Rikyu was caught in a shower on a mountain path. He saw the road being washed by the rain and pebbles coming out here and there on the surface. He thought it quite interesting. He then had pebbles placed in his garden for the first time, and he said that pebbles were to be so placed.

"Even now, we have never recommended merely tossing pebbles about. However, without realizing this, some dare to scatter pebbles so roughly that it may be dangerous for old men, who are liable to slip on them beside the hand-washing basin. Others even want to set the drain in a depression, and to place the front stone so far away from the basin as to make it difficult to reach the ladle. There is surely no difference between the length of the ancients' arms and that of modern men's." So he said and laughed.

26. Garden wash-basin and a ladle.

71. The Nasu Chaire

Meibutsu are rather rare among *nasu chaire* tea caddies. But the following are especially well known in the world: Somei *nasu*, Kitano *nasubi*, Daigo *nasu*, Bungo *nasubi*, *miotsukushi nasu*, Jo-o *nasubi*, Kyogoku *nasu* (this is said to have a dew design at its center), Hyogo *nasubi*, and others.

*

nasu or *nasubi*: lit., "eggplant," hence a *chaire* of that shape *(p. 71)*
Somei, etc.: names of places and tea aficionados
miotsukushi: "water-channel mark(s)"

72. The Hotei Chaire

The *hotei chaire* possessed by Rikyu was very famous. It is said to have been made in Bizen Province.

*

hotei: lit., "cloth bag." Rikyu so named the *chaire* because its bag was finer than the *chaire* itself. It also refers to Hotei, one of the seven gods of good luck, who carries a bag containing daily necessities.
Bizen Province: Okayama Prefecture at present

73. The Chidori Incense-Burner

Sogi liked incense and always retained its perfume in his beard. His incense burner was called the *chidori* incense-burner. Rikyu had bought it from someone at a price of a thousand *kan*. He loved it deeply, so his wife, So-on, asked him to show it to her. She gazed at it for a while, and said that it was 1 *bu* (3 mm.) too tall, and so it was not well shaped. She advised him to cut it shorter. Rikyu replied, "Well said! I was thinking the same thing myself." Then he called in a jewel polisher and asked him to cut it 1 *bu* shorter.

On the night of the fifteenth day of the eighth month, when the beams of the harvest moon were flooding the garden, Lord Yusai and Gamo Ujisato were served tea by Rikyu. After the tea, Ujisato asked Rikyu to show him the *chidori* incense burner. Rikyu behaved as if he were uninterested in it. He took out the incense burner, swept away the ash inside, and rolled it across to Ujisato. Yusai suggested that Rikyu's behavior might be due a connotation of the poem about Kiyomigata. On hearing that, Rikyu recovered from his displeasure and said, smiling, "That is it indeed!" This poem was composed by Emperor Juntoku:

> The beach of Kiyomigata:
> On the wave no cloud is reflected,
> But plovers flock and blur the moon.

Sogi (1421–1502): master of *renga*
chidori: lit., "plover," a bird with an unsteady gait, hence an incense burner resembling a tottering plover; *meibutsu*
Gamo Ujisato (1556–95): feudal lord and disciple of Rikyu
Kiyomigata: beach in Shizuoka Prefecture
Emperor Juntoku: r. 1210–21

74. The Utsumi Chaire

The *utsumi chaire* were formerly displayed on the *daisu*, but there was no precedent for using them in the small tearoom. A *meibutsu nasu katatsuki* tea caddy was always accompanied by one *utsumi* caddy to hold extra powdered tea in reserve. Rikyu thought it dangerous to place ceramic tea caddies close together, so instead of ceramic *utsumi* he used *mentori natsume* of lacquer ware. Nowadays the latter are called *seppu*, it is said.

*

utsumi: wide-mouthed *chaire*, called *utsumi* (inland sea) because smaller than the wide-mouthed *taikai* (ocean) *chaire* (p. 71)
mentori: lit., "beveled-edge" *natsume*
seppu: *natsume* with beveled (*mentori*) top and bottom edges, making it hard to tell top from bottom, as it is difficult to distinguish things in a snow storm (*fubuki* or *seppu*); used in this case for *koicha*

MENTORI   **SEPPU or FUBUKI**

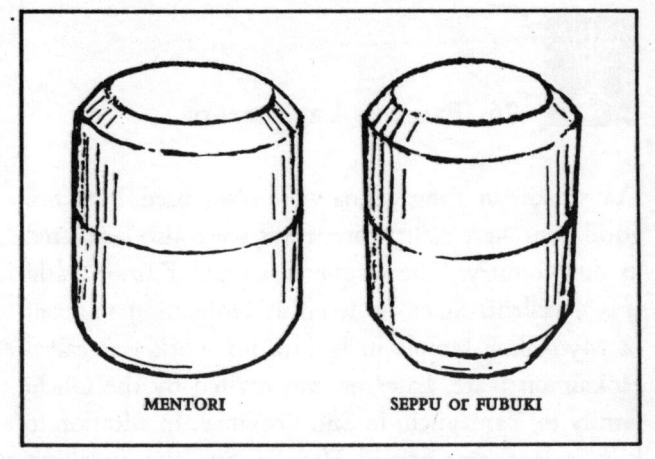

27. Lacquer tea caddies.

75. The Yuto Chaire

The *yuto chaire* at Yakushi-in in Sakai was a *meibutsu*. Later this tea caddy was handed down to Lord Akai Bungo-no-kami. It was imported, and had a handle attached above the mouth so that it could be carried about. The lid was just like that of a hand pail, and was in two parts, made so as to fit together at the joint.

*

yuto: lit., "hot-water jug" or "pail"

76. Famous Lacquerers

Trays made in Tang China were often used, but since good ones were rather rare, trays were also lacquered in our country. The lacquerer named Kamobayashi was excellent. Since he lived at Hokaimon in front of Myokakuji temple in Kyoto, his work was called Hokaimon ware. Later he was invited by the Ouchi family to Yamaguchi in Suo Province. In addition to him, a lacquerer named Haneda was also excellent. He is said to have lived in front of Daitokuji temple.

*

Tang dynasty: 618–907
Suo Province: Yamaguchi Prefecture at present
Haneda: Haneda Goro (*ca.* 1400)

77. The Uchiaka Trays

The *uchiaka* trays which are *meibutsu* were made in Tang China. "Yingchuan Dongfang" is written on them in cinnabar. Furthermore, the inscription "Made by Zhang Cheng" is carved on them with the point of a needle. In former days there existed seven of these trays, but the locations of those still in existence are as follows. Oda Uraku had two trays, but he sent one of them to some nobleman, and bequeathed the other to Oda Sangoro. One tray was preserved by another lord. One tray is said to be possessed by someone in Honganji temple.

*

uchiaka: tray usually lacquered red inside and green outside
Yingchuan Dongfang: Chinese engraver
Zhang Cheng (*ca.* 1300): Chinese master of cinnabar inscription
Oda Sangoro: Oda Nagayoshi, grandson of Oda Uraku; feudal lord and possessor of many *meibutsu*
Honganji: large temple in Kyoto

78. A List of Temmoku Bowls

A general list of *temmoku* tea bowls follows: *haikatsugi, yohen, yuteki, ki-temmoku, tada-temmoku, shiro-temmoku, kuiresan, kensan, ki-temmoku no shiro-temmoku, shiro-temmoku no ki-temmoku*.

*

haikatsugi: *temmoku* with a spotted design like falling ash
yohen: has spots of blue, yellow, purple, etc., against a black background
yuteki: like drops of oil scattered on water

ki-temmoku: lit., "yellow *temmoku*"
tada-temmoku: "ordinary *temmoku*"
shiro-temmoku: "white *temmoku*"
kuiresan: looks like a tortoise shell
kensan: small bowl made in the Jian (Japanese: Ken) area of China.
All the above are Chinese.

79. Temmoku Stands

The stands for *temmoku* tea bowls called the *nanatsu-dai* were *meibutsu*. They were made in Tang China. There were originally ten of them among the utensils in Zenkyo-an monastery, which was in Kenninji temple at Higashiyama, Kyoto. Three of them were lost, and seven remained. In the middle ages (*ca.* 1400–1600) Shinno discovered them and they became *meibutsu*. They were also called the *kazuno-dai*. According to another opinion, they were called Uruma-dai. There was another kind of *temmoku* stand, which was also *meibutsu* ranked just below the *kazuno-dai*, and much appreciated. When a Chinese ship came to Amagasaki in Settsu Province, ten stands came off it. The size was no different from that of the *kazuno-dai*. They were lacquered black, and each one had a drawing of a centipede in cinnabar 1 *sun* 1 *bu* 8 *rin* (4 cm.) in size. Therefore they were called the *mukade-dai*.

*

nanatsu-dai: lit., "seven stands"
kazuno-dai: "number stands"
Uruma-dai: "stands of Uruma," a temple
mukade-dai: "centipede stands"

80. The Shino Tea-Whisk Stand

Among the tea-whisk stands, there was a *meibutsu* known as Shino. This shallow bowl was made of white porcelain. It was a rough-textured piece with an allover network design, and the edge was shaped into a five-petaled flower. No one knows where it is now.

28. Tea-whisk stand, holding the tea whisk and chakin cloth.

[113]

81. The Hasami-chawan

The *hasami-chawan* is a tea-whisk stand, and it too is a *meibutsu*. There is a large crack in this celadon bowl, which is held together with brass clamps in two places, so cleverly that the clamps cannot be seen from the inside. It is indeed a most wonderful craftwork. Formerly it was possessed by Dosan, a doctor, and later it was transferred to Lord Uraku, who bequeathed it to Lord Sangoro, so it is said.

*

hasami-chawan: lit., "clamped bowl"

82. The Tea Scoop

The parts of the tea scoop are as follows: the pointed tip is called *tsuyu*, and the bottom end is *hasaki*. The portion with which tea powder is scooped up is generally called *sajikata* or *kaisaki*. When there is a gutter depressed in a line at the center, it is called *ubahi*. When there is a raised line at the center, with a depression in the front, it is called *ryohi*. There is a type of tea scoop which has a bamboo joint at the end on both sides, inside and outside; another without joints; and another with a single joint at the end of the handle. The tea scoops of Sosa II have such joints.

茶窓閑話

*

tsuyu: lit., "dewdrop"
hasaki: "blade point"
sajikata: "spoon shape"
kaisaki: "oar end"
ubahi: "old conduit"
ryohi: "double conduit"

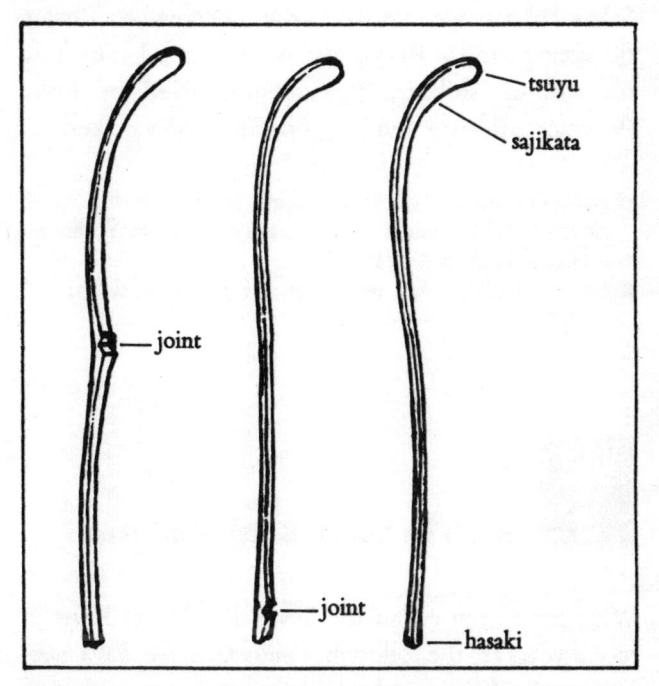

29. Various types of tea scoops; naming the parts and showing bamboo joints.

83. Makers of Tea Scoops

The makers of tea scoops are: Fukami Shutoku in the Higashiyama period, then Hanebuchi Hidehiro, then Shioze Muneyoshi. These three lived in Nara. Sosei, too, lived in Nara, at the same time as Jo-o. He was a well-known *wabisuki*, and very good at making tea scoops. Keishuza was a priest at Nansoji temple in Sakai. He was well versed in the tea ceremony during the same period as Rikyu, and was also good at making tea scoops. Ishikawa Rokuzaemon lived in Bishu Province, and was quite a good tea-scoop maker.

*

Higashiyama period: the late fifteenth century, during which the arts flourished under the patronage of Ashikaga Yoshimasa at Higashiyama in Kyoto
Keishuza: Nambo Sokei, tea master and disciple of Rikyu

84. The Seven Kettle-Lid Rests

What have been called the Seven Kettle-Lid Rests in recent years are the following: *mitsuba*, *sazae*, *hoya koro*, *kani*, *sannin bozu*, *gotoku*, and *wa*.

*

mitsuba: lit., "trefoil"
sazae: "turbo" or "turban shell"
hoya koro: "globular incense burner"
kani: "crab"
sannin bozu: "three priests"
gotoku: "trivet"
wa: "ring"

茶窓閒話

MITSUBA

BAMBOO

KANI

SAZAE

IKKANJIN

HOYA KORO

30. Selection of kettle-lid rests.

[117]

85. Sotan's Gourd

Among Sotan's works is a flower container made from a gourd. On its back is an inscription to Bodhidharma, and this comic poem:

> There is a reason
> A gourd becomes Bodhidharma:
> It is light enough
> To ride on a reed leaf.

*

Bodhidharma (or Daruma): great Indian priest, who introduced Zen to China in the sixth century, and was so enlightened that his daily life was as light and free as a dried gourd or reed leaf floating on the wind

86. Ichio Iori

Ichio Iori was a staff officer, and mastered the tea ceremony according to the instruction of Lord Sansai. He was very healthy and never suffered from even a headache until he was over sixty years old. Iori died of illness at the age of eighty-nine, on the thirteenth day of the eighth month in the second year of the Genroku era (1689). He was an expert on the tea ceremony in general, and also clever at craftworks. He made many tea scoops and flower containers. He wrote his name as Ichian 一庵, which is also pronounced *ichi iori*. He was fond of playing the *biwa,* and it is reported that he made a hundred of them.

茶窓閒話

*

Ichian: lit., "one hermitage"
biwa: Japanese lute

87. Sources of Charcoal

What is called Ikeda charcoal was produced not at Ikeda, but at Ichikura in the Tada section of Settsu Province, and then sent to Ikeda. From Ikeda it was delivered to various places. Therefore it came to be called Ikeda charcoal, though actually it should have been called Ichikura charcoal. Since the old days it has been recognized to be the charcoal best suited to the tea ceremony. But in the case of *wabicha,* Ono charcoal and Kurama charcoal were used in Kyoto, Iga charcoal in Mino and Owari Provinces, and Sakura charcoal in the Kanto district. The charcoal is actually used after being cut to size, and moistened in the rain. White charcoal has been made at Yokoyama in Izumi Province since ancient times. As it did not soil the hands of noblemen and noblewomen, it was used at court. This is a poem from the *Man'yoshu*:

> How and in what way
> Is Yokoyama charcoal
> Burned in Izumi Province
> So white in color?

This is a poem by Lord Teika:

> Yokoyama charcoal
> In Izumi Province
> Is so white in color
> That it stains nothing
> And there is nothing to say.

White charcoal is also made at Chihaya in Kawachi Province, as well as in the valley of Kotakidera in the same province, so this is now called Ko-no-taki charcoal.

*

wabicha: simple form of the tea ceremony, perfected by Rikyu
Ono: town in Hyogo Prefecture
Kurama: mountain and temple near Kyoto
Iga charcoal: actually Ise charcoal, of Ise in Mie Prefecture
Mino Province: Gifu Prefecture at present
Owari Province: Aichi Prefecture at present
Sakura: town in Chiba Prefecture
Man'yoshu: oldest anthology of Japanese poetry, compiled in the eighth century
Teika: Fujiwara no Sadaie (d. 1241), great poet, whose calligraphy was prized by tea connoisseurs
Kawachi Province: Osaka Prefecture at present

88. The Unselfishness of Rikyu

When Lord Nobunaga asked Rikyu about a *katatsuki chaire,* he answered that Tsuda Sokyu possessed a good one. Rikyu recommended it even though he was not on good terms with Sokyu. At once the lord purchased it, paying an unexpectedly large sum of gold to Sokyu. In return Sokyu sent barrels of wine, fish, gold, and other gifts to Rikyu. When Rikyu saw the messenger he said, "I only answered what I was asked. No prejudice should be at work in the case of *chaire,* and there is no cause for change in our bad relations. Therefore, I can find no reason to be given these gifts." So saying, he let the messenger return with the gifts.

*

Tsuda Sokyu (d. 1591): merchant, considered one of the three greatest tea masters, with Rikyu and Imai Sokyu

89. The Tsutsui Bowl

Lord Hideyoshi treasured his Ido tea bowl, but one of his pages dropped it and it broke into five pieces. The lord was very much displeased. Lord Yusai, who happened to be there, composed a poem on the spot and recited it:

> Tsutsui's bowl
> Broke into five pieces.
> The blame lies
> With none but me.

Hideyoshi was very impressed by this poem. It is said that since then the bowl has come to be called the Tsutsui bowl.

*

Ido: type of Korean tea bowl, possibly named for someone who owned many of them

Tsutsui: previous owner of this *meibutsu* bowl. The poem makes a play on Tsutsui and *itsutsu* (five).

31. An Ido tea bowl.

90. The Retired Emperor Views Tea Utensils

During the Genki era (1570–73), Retired Emperor Ogimachi requested that Rikyu show him a series of tea utensils. They were as follows: there were two *natsume*, one large and one small, both lacquered black. A full chrysanthemum was faintly painted in gold powder on the lid of the large one, and the outline of a paulownia on the small one. There was a tea scoop of ivory. The fresh-water vessel was a carved work of cedar. The incense container was made from a clam shell, and colored with gold both inside and out. A large white chrysanthemum was done in relief with powder on both the upper and the lower shells. The charcoal container was made of peeled cypress bark, with raised edges, and a large white chrysanthemum painted in the richest coloring. The bamboo flower container had two side openings, and the cut edges, the inside, and the bottom—but not the outer surface—were all lacquered with genuine black lacquer. A design of sea waves was done in metal flecks on the lacquered part. All the other utensils were ordinary ones. These utensils were shown and greatly appreciated. All were heartily welcomed and accepted with deep satisfaction. Rikyu was given the title of *koji* as a reward.

Retired Emperor Ogimachi: r. 1557–86; actually on the throne during the Genki era
koji: scholar out of government service, or simply a virtuous man

91. Tsuen's Calligraphy

This is the death ode of Tsuen of Uji:

> One bowl, one taste, in life;
> Last resolution, the cloud
> Is floating freely in the sky.
>
> The destination, the destination is nothing;
> If the thread is broken,
> It is only a piece of wood.

Ikenishi Gonsui, a *haikai* poet of Kyoto, happened to buy a sheet of paper on which this was written, and showed it to Soken at Shinjuan monastery in Daitokuji temple. Soken contemplated it for a while and said, "Well, well. This is indeed a strange thing, isn't it? Is it for sale?"

Gonsui answered, "It is merely an acquisition."

Soken said, "Then please sell it to me, as I love it very much. I am now seeing it for the first time, but truly it was written by Tsuen himself. At present I have no money available, so why not exchange it for the scroll hanging in the alcove? That is an oblong scroll done by Sesshu. It was once requested by Goto San'emon, but I did not sell it to him. Please take it with you in exchange. You may sell it to San'emon, but do not sell it to anyone else."

Gonsui did not believe all this to be true, and only laughed, saying, "You must have seen Tsuen's writings very often, mustn't you? How interested you look!"

Soken said, "No, this is not a joke at all. I would really like to have it in exchange for that scroll, so you may take the scroll down and go home with it."

Gonsui was very surprised but he took the scroll, saying, "Then I will have it."

Gonsui then stopped in at San'emon's house and showed him the scroll. When San'emon had a glimpse of it, he said, "How did you happen to bring it here? This is the very scroll that I saw at Shinjuan the other day and asked for. Did you really obtain it? I want to have it by all means."

Gonsui said, "Yes, I now see that you really want it. Soken said that this should not be sold to anyone other than you. As I got it in exchange for something else, I have brought it here to you at once."

San'emon was very happy and said, "Please leave it here. I should pay you one hundred *ryo*, but I must ask you to allow some discount, because I have spent a great deal of money on other utensils and I am now pressed for funds." So saying he handed Gonsui eighty *ryo*.

Gonsui often dealt with tea utensils, and was fond of the tea ceremony, too. This calligraphy by Tsuen and Daito's scroll were the two most valuable finds in his life. Tsuen's calligraphy was one of the most valuable scrolls in the world, so it was displayed at every tea ceremony held by Soken. It is said to be treasured in Shinjuan even now.

*

Tsuen: tea master
Uji: city near Kyoto famous for the production of tea
Ikenishi Gonsui (1650–1722): tea aficionado and *haikai* master
haikai: informal verse which evolved into haiku
Soken: Shinjuan Soken (1646–1715), *haikai* master
Goto San'emon: tea connoisseur
Daito: Shuho Myoto (1282–1337), also known as Daito Kokushi; great Zen priest and calligrapher, and founder of Daitokuji temple

92. A Leaf of Brushwood

Among Rikyu's writings, the one which is best known is a comment about a leaf of brushwood. It is this:

Teika's calligraphy on a small *shikishi* was

shown to me. This does not suit the nobleman's house. Even a leaf of brushwood can be properly appreciated by a man who enjoys tea.

*

shikishi: square of fine paper for calligraphy, which was mounted on a scroll to be hung in the tearoom

93. Rikyu's Daughter

Osan, Rikyu's daughter, married Mozuya and had a son by him, but a little later she was widowed while still in her youth. Now, in the spring of the eighteenth year of the Tensho era (1591), Lord Hideyoshi visited many feudal lords at their homes, because the country had become peaceful and quiet. Tea ceremonies were often held, and Noh plays performed. He also went out to enjoy falconry from time to time.

At the beginning of the third month, Hideyoshi went out as far as Higashiyama and its vicinity to enjoy a bit of falconry. On the way he passed by the front of Nanzenji temple, and then through the neighborhood of Kurodani valley. He was accompanied by the warriors Sasa Awaji-no-kami, Maeba Hannyu, and Kinoshita Hansuke, and also three pages.

32. A woman accompanied by some maids came strolling along,

looking at the flowers, with her palanquin following behind her.

He set his hawk himself, and then happened to come to a narrow passage on a mountain road. Just there a woman was coming by, accompanied by two or three maids, with her palanquin following behind her. A humble-looking manservant was carrying a box that looked like luncheon on his shoulder. The woman came strolling quietly along, looking up at the flowers on the mountain treetops.

Kinoshita Hansuke stepped before Hideyoshi, raised his fan, and cried out, "Our honorable lord is coming! Take off your hats and hoods!" The menservants put the palanquin aside in a rice field, and lowered their heads to the ground. The woman looked a little surprised, but not perturbed, and took off her hood, leaving only her forehead covering in place. She stepped aside under the shade of a tree full of flowers in bloom. Hideyoshi gazed at her. She seemed to be a little over thirty years of age. She wore a padded garment of white silk, with folds of red silk inside, and on the outside a purple covering stitched with gold thread. Her waist was lithe and graceful. She picked up the hem of her long dress a little, and tried to hide herself under the flowers, glancing shyly toward the lord. Her charming eyes and face could not have been equaled by the beauty of any flower.

Not only Hideyoshi but also all his attendants were overcome by her beauty, and their hearts beat fast. One of the pages was ordered to ask who she was. A maid accompanying her answered that she was the daughter of Rikyu and widow of Mozuya. The lord said to himself that he had heard tell of her beauty, and now found her to be truly as lovely as had been reported, for indeed no court lady could surpass her in beauty.

Later Hideyoshi sent her an amorous letter, calling her to his Jurakudai palace. But she did not answer his letter, as she had only recently been bereaved of her husband and was still in tears of mourning with her infant boy. Therefore, she sincerely wished to be excused, and she did not write any answer to the lord.

But Hideyoshi's infatuation and longing for her increased more and more. He sent the warrior Tonda Sakon as a private messenger to Rikyu, her father, repeatedly requesting him to send his daughter to serve at the Jurakudai palace. However, Rikyu found it difficult to force his daughter to violate her chastity, and he also disliked the idea of sending his own daughter to the lord as a concubine. He was also afraid that he might be thought to be trying to pander to the lord in order to attain special favor. Finally he decided not to accept the request. Hideyoshi himself could not violate the rules of public decorum, and yet he felt quite frustrated. Indeed, deep in his mind, he was very indignant.

It happened that the tower gate of Daitokuji temple was rebuilt, and when the ridge plate was installed, a wooden statue of Rikyu was mounted on it. This was already well known in the world, but when it reached Hideyoshi's ears, he was moved to the height of fury against Rikyu's excessive conceit. In addition, some wicked vassals found this a good opportunity to repeatedly tell slanderous tales against Rikyu—of his self-interest in the evaluation of utensils, his receiving bribes for recommending persons to Hideyoshi, and so on. It is said that Hideyoshi might otherwise have considered the situation more prudently, but since he had previously had unsatisfactory experiences with Rikyu, he put Rikyu to death after all.

The tower gate of Daitokuji temple was originally constructed by Socho, a *renga* poet, but in the course of the years it decayed. When Rikyu became wealthy, he consulted Sochin, a representative supporter of the temple, and offered his help to the priest Kokei. The tower gate was thus reconstructed. The ridge plate was installed and the wooden statue made. The statue wore a wadded silk garment with a paulownia crest, and an outer garment of silk crepe. On its head a horned hood leaned to the right. It had worn-out sandals on its feet, and held a stick which was stuck in the ground. Its eyes were looking afar. This statue was positioned up on the tower. It is said that there were some accusations after this affair, but Sochin took the whole blame and punishment on himself, so that nothing was blamed on Daitokuji temple.

*

Nanzenji temple, Kurodani valley, Jurakudai palace: all in Kyoto
Socho (1448–1532): noted *renga* poet

94. The Legacy of Rikyu's House

It is said that the reception room of Rikyu's house was made into a tearoom at Kotoin, a branch of Daitokuji temple. The front gate was made into the gate of Ryokoin, another branch of the same temple. The kitchen gate was moved to Myorenji temple of the Nichiren sect to be rebuilt there.

95. Sansai's Stone Lantern

Rikyu gave Lord Sansai his Amida-do kettle, *hachi-hiraki* tea bowl, and stone lantern. Throughout Sansai's life never a day passed without his seeing and enjoying this kettle and this bowl. He used them lovingly at every tea ceremony. He placed the stone lantern in the garden of his living room. When he went on a trip to other provinces, he took it with him and had it put in

33. Stone lantern in a garden.

place and lighted at every overnight stay in order to enjoy it. Early the following morning the man in charge of the tea ceremony carried it to the next stop, placed it at the most appropriate spot during the daytime before the lord's arrival, and then lighted it. After the death of Sansai, this lantern was donated to Kotoin in Daitokuji temple, and made into his tombstone. In addition, the Amida-do kettle was handed down to Nagaoka Kyumu. It was said laughingly that Amida had fallen down to hell.

*

Amida-do: lit., "temple of Amida" Buddha, at Arima near Kobe, where Rikyu found this kettle *(p. 35)*
hachihiraki: "open bowl" or wide-mouthed bowl
Nagaoka Kyumu: relative of Sansai. The joke hinges on the fall of the kettle from a master like Rikyu to a lesser tea connoisseur like Kyumu.

96. Rikyu's Principal Disciples

Among all the disciples of Rikyu, the so-called seven principal disciples were: Oda Uraku, Gamo Ujisato, Hosokawa Sansai, Seta Masatada, Shibayama Kemmotsu, and Takayama Ukon. One opinion holds that Uraku should be excluded and Sakuma Fukan included. And another view is said to have excluded both Uraku and Fukan, and included Arima Gemba.

*

Seta Masatada: feudal lord
Shibayama Kemmotsu: Shibayama Munetsune, vassal of Nobunaga and Hideyoshi
Sakuma Fukan: Sakuma Masakatsu (1556–1631), feudal lord
Arima Gemba: Arima Toyouji (1570–1642), feudal lord

97. Schools of the Tea Ceremony

In former days, up to the time of Sen no Rikyu, there still lived several tea masters of old schools. Among them Tsuda Sokyu, Imai Sokyu, and others were the outstanding masters. There were many other famous tea connoisseurs in addition to them who were not related to the Sen family. No one knows when the old schools declined one after another so that they only remained nominally. On the other hand, the Sen family alone grew more and more prosperous. Below are the independent schools in the present world, but all have come out of the Sen family as their root. Indeed the Sen family as a whole can justly be called the grand masters of the tea ceremony. The independent schools are those of Sansai, Furuori, Uraku, Enshu,

Ichio, Sakuma, Funakoshi, Taga, Kanamori, Katagiri, Sadaoki, Sohen, and so on.

*

Furuori: Furuta Oribe (1544–1615)
Funakoshi: Funakoshi Iyo (1598–1671)
Taga: Taga Sakon (d. 1657)
Katagiri: Katagiri Sekishu (1605–73)
Sadaoki: Oda Sadaoki (1618–1706)
Sohen: Yamada Sohen (1628–1708)

98. The Tea Competition

In the book *Taiheiki*, Sasaki Doyo celebrated the festival of Tanabata. He decorated seven plates, had seven dishes cooked, collected seven hundred kinds of prizes, and prepared seventy bowls of tea. Then he invited the honorable prime minister to distinguish the authentic tea from the inauthentic teas by drinking them. He got this idea from the art of distinguishing different kinds of incense, and he considered Togano-o tea to be authentic while teas produced elsewhere were inauthentic. All these teas were served one after another at random. Each participant drank each tea and tried to distinguish the authentic tea from the inauthentic ones, recording the result. It is said that all competed with one another, and those who made correct guesses were given prizes.

*

Sasaki Doyo: Sasaki Takauji (1295–1373), feudal lord, poet, and expert on incense

Tanabata: Star Festival, held on the seventh day of the seventh month, hence the repeated sevens

99. Chakabuki

In the "Record of Ten Bowls of Tea," the priest Gyoyo mentions *kaicha* or *yocha*. *Kaicha* was named with reference to the saying "The *kaisha* hears one and knows ten, while his guest hears one and knows two." *Kaicha* originally came from someone's turning the game of authentic or inauthentic tea into a so-called elegant performance. This is not the regular procedure of the tea ceremony. Thinking thus, Sotan nicknamed it *chakabuki*, and he never used it.

*

Gyoyo: priest who made a compilation called *Ainosho* (1446) containing the "Record of Ten Bowls of Tea"

kaicha or *yocha*: way of taking tea in turn

kaisha: host

100. The Unzan Katatsuki

There lived a man at Sakai who had a Chinese *meibutsu katatsuki* with the name of Unzan. He invited Rikyu and served him tea with that caddy, but Rikyu showed no interest in it at all. After Rikyu left, the host felt that any *katatsuki* which Rikyu did not praise could not be a good one, so he threw it against the trivet and it cracked. Those who happened to be present remarked to themselves how short-tempered he was, and obtained the cracked utensil and took it away. They repaired it themselves, and then displayed it at a tea gathering, inviting Rikyu as a guest. When Rikyu saw it he said that it must be the very Unzan that he had seen a few days earlier and, contrary to their expectations, he admired it. Thereupon it was hurriedly returned to its former owner with a report of the event.

Afterward the Unzan was passed on to different persons in turn, until finally it came into the possession of a certain lord. A doctor heard that Lord Kyogoku had been wanting the Unzan very badly, so the doctor went to the lord who possessed it and had a talk with him about the tea ceremony. In the course of the conversation, the doctor said that Kyogoku had such a strong longing for the Unzan that he often declared he did not desire any other *chaire* in all his life. On hearing this, the possessor said with rather a laugh, as if it were some joke, that since the Unzan was so eagerly desired he might sell it. But only one load of gold would be too cheap a price; two loads would be necessary to get him to sell it.

The doctor went to Kyogoku at once to report the conversation. When Kyogoku heard it, he asked the doctor if what he reported was true. When the doctor answered with conviction that he had really been there and talked directly to the possessor, Kyogoku requested him to purchase the Unzan for two loads of gold. The doctor immediately accepted the task of negotiating the transaction.

But next the possessor said that his previous comment had been only a joke, and that actually he had no intention of selling the Unzan at any price. The doctor was put in a most difficult position. The possessor would never consent to sell it, while Kyogoku, too, would never give up on it. The affair had turned out to be a great problem.

At this point some other people tried to arrange a compromise and mediate the affair, strongly pressuring the possessor. At last he understood the situation and sold the Unzan to Kyogoku at the price of two loads of gold. The reason the possessor agreed was that the harvest in his territory had been a failure, and so this money was to be shared out to help the peasants. When the situation was reported to him privately, he sold the Unzan at last to Kyogoku. The gold in the two loads was said to total about twelve thousand *ryo*. Kyogoku was very pleased indeed.

One day Kyogoku showed the Unzan to Enshu and said, "The parts do not fit together well in places, and it looks rather ugly. What would you think of having it repaired again?"

Enshu answered, "The improper fit itself is rather interesting, and Rikyu admired it as attractive, so that it came to be famous. It is a *meibutsu* as it is."

In recent years, a cracked bowl has often been used after being repaired, but a *chaire* is never used once it has been damaged, to say nothing of broken, even after being repaired. But one must make a decision according to the nature of the object itself. In the case of a *meibutsu* imported from Tang China, it may be quite all right to use it after repairing a broken or cracked part.

*

Kyogoku: Kyogoku Takahiro Anchi (1599–1677), feudal lord and tea aficionado

101. Tea and the Seasons

Rikyu held the ceremony of opening the tea-leaf jar when the citrons changed color. Sotan said that it is good to hold the tea ceremony with the brazier when the fir trees sprout fresh needles.

102. The Food of the Tea Gathering

It is said that at tea gatherings in the age of Rikyu, three kinds of vegetables, three bottles of sakè, and one kind of fish were usually served.

103. The Stones by the Basin

The stones at the drain by the garden basin are to be stocked in a container, and then scattered about at random. This is to be done by a servant with his eyes closed. However, it is good to show him with a stick how to rearrange those which go astray. It is not good

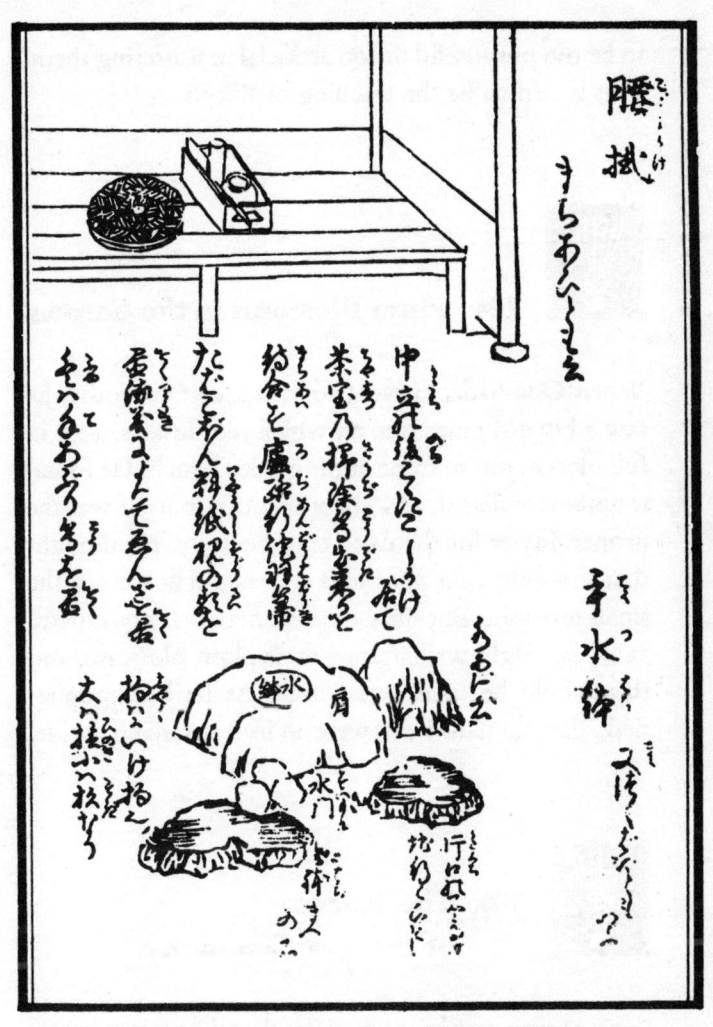

34. Stones at the drain by the garden basin. *Above:* a waiting bench, with a straw cushion and a tobacco set for the guests.

to be too purposeful or too artificial in scattering them. This is said to be the teaching of Rikyu.

104. Plum Blossoms in the Garden

When Oda Sadaoki went to visit a certain house, he saw a big old plum tree on which red flowers were in full bloom, just in front of the garden bench. He found it quite wonderful, and knew that this in itself was the proper flower for the day's tea ceremony. He thought that it would be a poor idea to arrange flowers in the small tearoom. But since the host here was not tasteful at all, he might well arrange these plum blossoms, and that would be tastelessness itself. As he had prophesied, the plum flowers were indeed arranged inside.

105. The Essence of the Tea Ceremony

Sotan always taught his disciples that the tea ceremony should be like a discussion of Zen, and therefore there would be no book of recorded secrets. But what had been really understood or mastered was said to be written as the testament of the *itomaki*. On the other hand, Lord Nobunaga and Lord Hideyoshi liked the tea ceremony because to them it had some other inexpressible meaning. The deepest principle or essence was said to have been told by Sohen to Takeshita Heigaku in confidence.

*

itomaki: lit., "spool," suggesting that the teachings of the tea masters form a thread which is preserved as if wound up on a spool

106. The Tea Connoisseur's Single-Heartedness

One day in battle, Lord Mitsuhide and Lord Hisahide took up positions and united their forces by the order of Lord Nobunaga. It happened that the position of Hisahide's unit was a little too far in advance of Mitsuhide's, so Mitsuhide explained that the other's position ought to be pulled back a bit. When Hisahide heard this he thanked Mitsuhide for his reasonable advice, but said, "You may be right, but for a man like myself who has been studying the tea ceremony for so many years, it is impossible to have two different ways of thinking. His position should be eliminated if necessary rather than being rearranged." So saying he did not rearrange his position after all, and yet he won the victory.

107. A Dispute Between Father and Son

Rikyu was hanging a kettle from a pothanger in a small tearoom with a central pillar, when Shoan came in and said that a pothanger was unsuitable for that room. Paying no attention to his son's comment, Rikyu went into the kitchen, saying, "Pothangers have been in common use since the old days, so anyone may use them. You say such impertinent things!"

108. The Imogashira Water Vessels

The *imogashira* fresh-water vessels were so called because their shape resembled that of a potato head. These porcelains were brought in by the Europeans, and were very rare in past days. None but Rikyu and

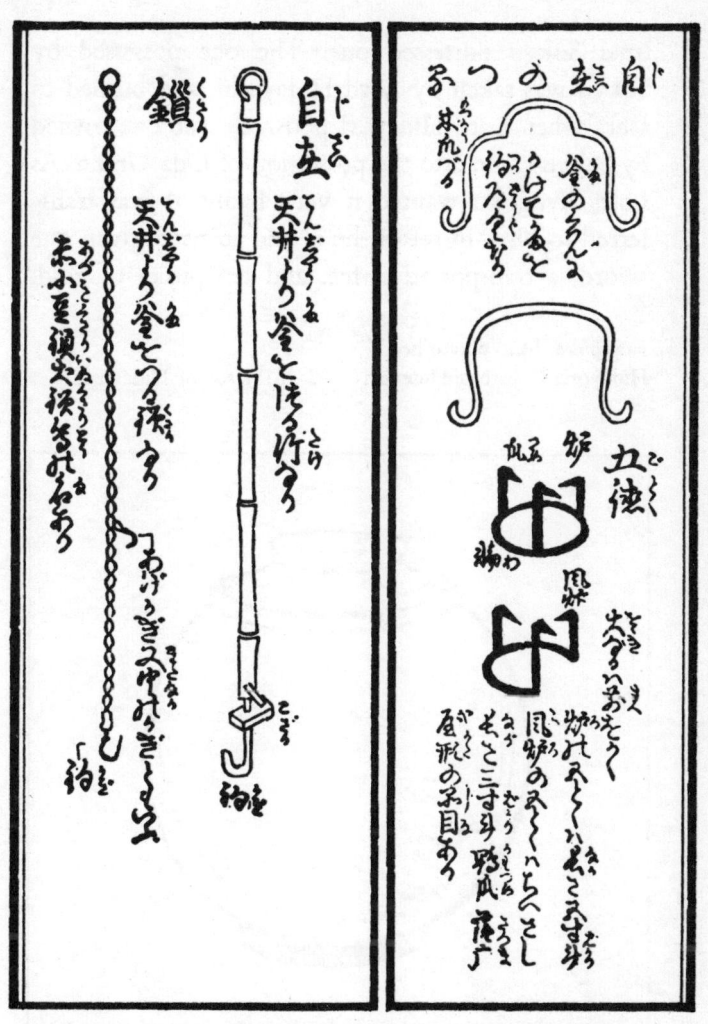

35. *Left:* pothangers from which kettle on kettle-ring hanger is suspended. *Right:* two designs of kettle-ring hangers, and trivets.

Imai Sokyu possessed one. The one possessed by Sokyu was taken by Lord Hideyoshi, and burned to ashes when Lord Hideyori perished. The one owned by Rikyu came into the possession of Oda Uraku. As Lord Kyogoku wanted it very badly, it was transferred to him. In return he is said to have given one sword, a transportation fee, and ten pieces of gold.

*

imogashira: lit., "potato head"
Hideyori: Toyotomi Hideyori (1593–1615), son of Hideyoshi

36. Imogashira water-jar.

37. Raku tea bowl.

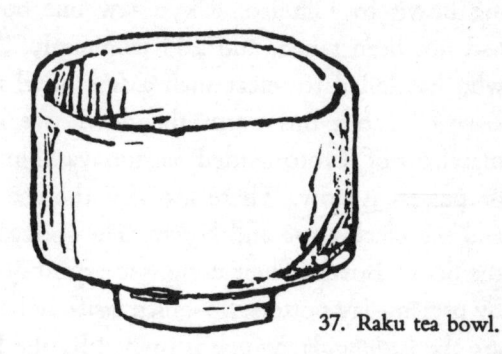

109. Raku Ware

A potter came to Japan from the country of Korea, and made tea bowls and other utensils. This is the origin of Raku ware. Taking the character 朝 *cho* from Chosen, the name of his native country, he called himself Chojiro, it is said. Among his bowls the following came to be *meibutsu*: first, the black Toyobo possessed by Toyobo. There was a man who wanted to buy it at a price of seven hundred gold *ryo*, but it is said that Toyobo did not sell it. Now a merchant in Osaka by the name of Konoike is said to possess it. The black Rinzai was said to be owned by Oda Shimofusa-no-kami. The *kimamori* was said to be owned by a certain lord in the western district. As to the *kengyo*, Rikyu and some other people were once selecting bowls by Chojiro. Rikyu saw one bowl which had not been taken, and said laughingly, "Everyone who has failed to select such a fine bowl must be a *kengyo*." From this event the bowl was named. A merchant of Kyoto named Satsumaya Shimbei is said to possess it now. There are also the red *hayabune*, and the black *oguro* and *koguro*. The above are called the Seven Bowls. Their designs are most often copied by present-day potters. So-called *meibutsu* besides these are the *hachihiraki*, which is owned by the Hosokawa family, and the *ayame*, *makomo*, *sairai*, *kankyo*, *ichimonji*, *tokabo*, Tarobo, and *nuregarasu*.

*

Chojiro: Tanaka Nagasuke (1516–89), famous potter
Rinzai: Zen priest and his sect
Oda Shimofusa-no-kami: probably Oda Nobukatsu Joshin (1558–1630), son of Nobunaga
kimamori: lit., "tree protector." A persimmon tree's best fruit was left on the tree to "protect" it and to bring good fruit the next year.
kengyo: "blind man"
hayabune: "fast ship"
oguro: "large black"
koguro: "small black"
ayame: "iris"
makomo: "reed"
sairai: "returning again"
kankyo: "retreat" or "retirement"
ichimonji: "straight line"
tokabo: "priest's peach-blossom residence"
Tarobo: "the priest Taro's residence"
nuregarasu: "wet crow"

110. Decorating the Shelf

It was Rikyu's preference that when a tearoom shelf is arranged, two *meibutsu* should never be displayed on it together.

111. The Konrinji Natsume

What Rikyu called Konrinji was a *natsume* of an unusual design. This tea caddy bore a representation of Mount Kasuga in raised gold lacquer, and the bag was of old gold brocade with a dark blue backing. It was made by order of Emperor Go-Daigo, and it is now treasured at Kissui-in temple in Yamato Province. One is also kept at Sakai. There are many people who possess imitations. One record states that it is the traditional practice to place the real Konrinji on a lacquered tray of pine-bark color and design before use. The design has been copied with a mulberry or a Chinese quince depicted by repeated thin lacquerings, it is said.

*

Konrinji: temple in Nara Prefecture where Emperor Go-Daigo
  had the first Konrinji *natsume* made
Mount Kasuga, Kissui-in temple: in Nara Prefecture
Emperor Go-Daigo: r. 1318–39

112. Sword-Sheath Design

Lord Sansai was skillful and talented in many fields. In particular, he established a school of sword-sheath design called the Etchu school, which is still very popular. But this school is not what it was at its establishment. It should rather be called the Rikyu school. The true story is as follows:

One day Rikyu visited Sansai's house and had an enjoyable conversation with him. Then Sansai said that he had had a very good sword sheath made, and he showed it to Rikyu. When Rikyu saw it he said, "A few days ago, I stopped by the shop of a dealer in various articles. There I discovered a sword sheath which I thought looked especially good among the numerous sheaths on display, so I bought it. That sheath is much better than this one of yours."

Sansai was surprised to hear this and said, "The design of this sheath has already become famous as the Etchu design, and is prized throughout the country.

[152]

Why do you say things like that? It disturbs me to hear of a better design for a sheath. Please show it to me at once." Immediately it was brought to him. He looked at it and found it to be far superior to his own. So he ceased using his old design and decided to adopt the new one, and ordered a sheath made on the new design.

Sansai told this story to Miyake Boyo. Then Sansai showed him a *kozuka* and said, "The design of this *kozuka* hilt is also Rikyu's favorite one. One day Rikyu saw my *kozuka* and asked who had engraved its hilt. So I answered that it was a *meibutsu,* the *kangen* hilt designed by Yujo. Rikyu said that it might be liked by people of the lower classes, but it was unsuitable for upper-class people, so I had better not use it. Then I asked Rikyu to make a suitable one for me. After a while Rikyu had one made and gave it to me. I treasure it now." So saying, Sansai showed it to Boyo. It was covered with pure silver on both sides. It had no conspicuous pattern or distinctive marking but was of simple and noble design. Boyo told this story some days later.

This Boyo was also a master of incense. He was taught about the use of incense in the tea ceremony by Sansai, who had received Rikyu's personal instruction in that art. Boyo taught it to Fujimura Yoken, and passed on his incense burner by the name of Tago-no-ura as a testimony of certification, so it is said.

38. Sansai showed Rikyu his highly prized sword-sheath.

[155]

Etchu: Sansai was lord of Etchu Province (Toyama Prefecture at present).
Miyake Boyo (1580–1649): great scholar, well versed in the arts
kozuka: dagger attached to a short-sword sheath
kangen: lit., "wind and string" musical instruments
Yujo (d. 1512): designer of swords and metal chasing
Fujimura Yoken (1613–99): disciple of Sotan

113. The Tea Ceremony for Warriors

Lord Sansai, one of the seven principal disciples of Rikyu, enjoyed a very long life. Therefore in his later years he came to be called "the one and only master of the tea ceremony." He was one of the great feudal lords, and had good taste in many areas. He was also very fond of the tea ceremony. Therefore he easily became friendly with many people, and had many disciples.

One day a young lord who was fond of the tea ceremony came to ask if he could be Sansai's disciple and learn the tea ceremony. Sansai accepted this request and promised to teach him thoroughly. "First of all," Sansai said, "you must fully understand the most important consideration for a warrior in the tea ceremony. Now that the tea ceremony has become prevalent in the world and is carefully studied and observed, people seem to have forgotten the vocation of their own clans. They try to imitate the ways of hermits or people who have retired from active life. While they try to discover Zen in a bowl of tea and enjoy solitude and tranquility, they are liable to ignore the military arts which are the indispensable requisites for their own lives. This is the current failing of the tea ceremony.

"Those who are fond of the tea ceremony should follow the examples set by Lord Nobunaga and Lord Hideyoshi, the most honorable lords of the highest position, and also by lesser persons such as Lord Ujisato and I myself. To begin with, the most important thing for any warrior is to devote himself wholly to the military arts day and night. If a military emergency should occur at any moment, he should be the first to present himself at the front, never arriving behind others and wasting no time in his preparations. At the front he should be ready to fight together with his own unit and beat off any enemy, even an enemy numbering thousands of horsemen. To make this possible, all his clan, even down to the servants of the lowest class, to say nothing of the fighting men and horses themselves, should always be trained in the military arts, neglecting no arm, weapon, nor element of horsemanship. All should be ready at a moment's notice. On the other hand, when he has time to spare, he may enjoy the solitary quietness and sublime beauty of the tea ceremony. Such is the point of the tea ceremony for warriors themselves.

"But now one goes to visit others who like tea at any time, either at night or in the morning. The host who receives such guests is always ready to meet surprise visitors and arranges things immediately, treating them with the utmost hospitality and serving them tea. It appears that he is well prepared in all ways. But when his preparations for warfare are carefully inspected, he is found to be not at all ready. He could not make himself ready to go out to the front even with ten or twenty days for preparation. His neglect could not be greater than this.

"I myself am now old and reduced to skin and bones, so that I can scarcely manage to handle the ladle. And yet years ago in the tenth month, when I was fifteen years old and my brother Tongoro was fourteen, we two attacked the enemy at the castle of Kataoka in Kawachi Province ahead of all the others. At that battle Lord Nobunaga gave us a commendation. Since then I have struck with the spear, cut off heads, and been bathed in blood innumerable times. Ujisato, too, a hero whom I can never hope to equal, has become great. Both of us rose up to become lords not through the power of the tea scoop, but through our efforts in our own vocation.

"If a lord holds to the principle of never forgetting his own inclination, then his inclination will become that of his thousands of followers. Both Lord Nobunaga and Lord Hideyoshi were fond of tea, so those whose names are known in the world practice the tea ceremony without exception. Consider this fact well. Either in the case of a great lord or that of a lesser lord, what the master likes is also liked by all his followers. Therefore the master's intentions are important. If you alone like tea, all your clansmen will come to like tea, too. If you like the military arts, your clansmen will not neglect the military arts.

"But there is one great distinction to be made here. If the master likes dancing or the tea ceremony, which are after all not indispensable to the clan, he is sure to be followed throughout the clan. On the other hand, if the master likes archery, horsemanship, or the other military arts, his followers' devotion will only be half as sincere as in the case of dancing or the tea ceremony. Therefore the warrior should make it a rule to consider this tendency seriously when he wishes to enjoy a pastime. We are now in an age of peace and tranquility, so you may never have to wade through blood, and yet you should train yourself with bamboo or wooden swords though it raises blisters on your palms, or engage in deer hunting or falconry though it makes your feet hurt. And after that you may handle the tea ladle.

"The other day a man came to me for tea instruction and said, 'If we know nothing about the tea ceremony, we are liable to be thought wild and unrefined, and to cause a party to be awkward and rustic. And I might feel myself to be rather funny and clumsy.'

"Then I asked him, 'How do you cut *kitsuki* on the battlefield?'

"He queried me back at once, 'What does *kitsuki* mean?'

"I told him, 'It means the way of cutting off a head with the helmet on.'

"He now answered, 'That is something I know well. First, I toss the helmet away, then I take up the disheveled hair, then I cut off the head.'

"His clever answer had been learned merely from Noh chant, not from actual experience on the battlefield. It disappointed me greatly, but as he was the son of an intimate friend, I taught him how to cut off a head in detail. After that I scolded him bitterly and advised him, 'If you do not know that *kitsuki* means cutting off a head, and yet you say that you must learn the tea ceremony, then you are foolish indeed. From now on you should devote yourself wholly to the military arts, and never think of learning the tea ceremony.'

"Then I told him a story. Many years ago, in the presence of Lord Hideyoshi, there was a discussion about the tea ceremony among the pages. They asked me how to tie the *chaire* bag and other questions of that kind. Among the pages was Hori Tango-no-kami Naoyori, who was about twelve or thirteen years old at that time. He said to me, 'My lord, please teach me how to securely tie the helmet string on the battlefield.'

"Clever was he indeed! This can be said to be the true tea ceremony for warriors. Very fine! This young boy had made the best remark there that day. I thought he would surely distinguish himself in the future. So I answered him, 'Well, of course. I will tell you what I remember.' Lord Hideyoshi, too, was put in extraordinarily good humor. And see how Tango-no-kami has been promoted since then.

"In any case, every warrior should have this kind of resolution uppermost in his mind. If a man should devote himself solely to the tea ceremony without this sublime resolution, and neglect his swords both long and short, he might as well become a mere tea server. Now I myself am very old, but if some conflict should arise, I might be summoned to teach the young people, as there are so many of them now. Therefore I am always ready to go out to the battlefront at any moment. This attitude may, I think, be called the true essence of the tea ceremony for warriors. Everyone should be very prudent indeed." This was Sansai's advice.

*

Tongoro: Hosokawa Okimoto (1562–1619), feudal lord

Part Two

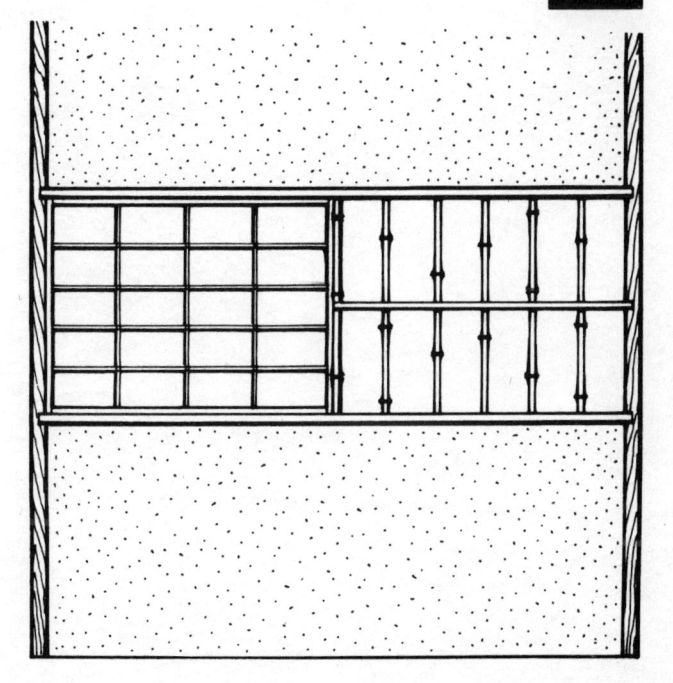

茶窓閒話

DURING THE Kambun era (1661–73), there lived a man named Emura Sogu. He was a man of Kyoto and was commonly called Sensai Sensei. His father's name was Kisai, and he was famous for *waka* and *renga* poetry, and was also a master of the art of incense. Sogu himself had a reputation as a scholar of Confucianism. When he reached the great age of one hundred, Emperor Go-Mizuno-o, who was on the throne at that time, summoned him to ask how he had developed and trained himself. The emperor gave him some gold, a *hatozue,* and other things. In the ninth month of that year several mushrooms grew up in Sogu's garden. This was considered to be a good omen. Three *waka* that he composed on New Year's Day that year have been handed down to us.

This old man often talked about what he had seen and heard during his one hundred years since the time of Lord Nobunaga. A man who was always beside him wrote down his stories and compiled them in two volumes, which he called *An Old Man's Tales*. Several of the stories have some connection with the tea ceremony. As there remain only a few copies of this book now, some of the stories have been selected and added on here. Sogu's words are truly just as they were actually recorded.

*

Emura Sogu (1565–1664): scholar and doctor, with the pen name of Kishoan
waka: thirty-one syllable poem
Emperor Go-Mizuno-o: r. 1611–29. Actually, the reigning emperor during the Kambun era was Go-Sai.
hatozue: pigeon-headed walking stick given to old men as a symbol of long life
An Old Man's Tales: Rojin Zatsuwa

39. Kikusui (chrysanthemum and water) crest-design.

114. The Kikusui Kettle

In the age of Lord Hideyoshi, there was a *meibutsu* kettle called the *kikusui* kettle. It bore a floating-chrysanthemum crest, and the mouth was so wide that there remained a shoulder of only 1 *sun* (3 cm.). This kettle had a covering lid like that of a brass or copper kettle. It was preserved by the Gamo family.

*

kikusui: lit., "chrysanthemum and water"

115. The Daikodo Kettle

The *daikodo* kettle, a *meibutsu*, was found on Mount Hiei. The characters 大講堂 *daikodo* were cast on the side of the kettle. It was destroyed by the fire in the year Hinoto-Tori (1597). The mouth of this kettle, too, was wide.

*

daikodo: lit., "auditorium"
Mount Hiei: site of Enryakuji temple, near Kyoto

116. Early Meibutsu

It is only in recent years that the price of *chaire* has grown expensive. When the Old Man, Emura Sogu, was a small boy, there were only two so-called *meibutsu* in the world: the Gyokudo *chaire,* and the *enza katatsuki* possessed by Rikyu. These two were priceless, and were treated as unequaled *meibutsu.* Later Furuta Oribe bought a Chinese *chaire.* It was named Shokokuji because it was found in Shokokuji temple. He bought it at a price of eleven pieces of gold. This was the first sale of a tea utensil for a high price. Soon afterward he sold it to the lord of Kaga Province for one thousand five hundred *kan.* This happened because Lord Oribe had to urgently make a payment to Lord Ishida Mitsunari, who had been pressing him. As Oribe was on bad terms with Mitsunari, he had to sell the *chaire* to raise funds to settle the accounts between them. Dotetsushi Enjobo acted as the agent, and the price was paid. The Old Man happened to be there with Oribe at the time. Sixty pieces of gold and a *rengeo* tea-leaf jar, which had been particularly requested, made up the payment. The *enza katatsuki* was kept in Edo, but it is said to have been destroyed in the fire of the year Hinoto-Tori (1597).

*

Gyokudo: priest who possessed this Chinese *chaire*
enza: lit., "round cushion"
Shokokuji: temple in Kyoto
Ishida Mitsunari (1560–1600): feudal lord and tea aficionado
Dotetsushi Enjobo: Enjobo Soen, priest and tea master; disciple of Rikyu
rengeo: "lotus king"; tea-leaf jar bearing a design of lotus petals and the character 王 "king"

117. The Hino Katatsuki

Before Hino Yuishin sold the Hino *katatsuki* to Daimonjiya, he called in the Old Man and said, 'I promised to sell this tea caddy at a price of fifty pieces of gold, but as there is something distasteful about it fifty *kan* can be deducted, and so the price will be forty-five pieces of gold. I want it to go to Mimasaka, if he desires it." He put it in his sleeve and showed it to Lord Mimasaka, but since the payment was not ready, it was not sold to him. At last it fell into the hands of Daimonjiya.

*

Daimonjiya: merchant and tea connoisseur
Mimasaka: lord of Mimasaka Province (Okayama Prefecture at present)

118. The Ogura Shikishi

The Ogura *shikishi* were originally possessed by the governor of Ise Province. All one hundred of them were pasted on a double-panel screen. When Socho, a disciple of Sogi, went down to Ise, the governor proposed to present the entire screen to Socho. Socho refused to accept the whole thing, but took just one panel. The other panel was burned to ashes by a fire at Ise. That one panel which remained safe with Socho is now very well known in the world, and about thirty of the *shikishi* exist at present. Jo-o was said to possess two of them: one with the poem "Amanohara" and one with "Yaemugura." These two are mounted as hanging scrolls.

The Old Man attended tea gatherings held by Doan, Rikyu's son, several years in succession. Doan arranged flowers in a container called *tsuru no hitokoe,* and he never once hung a scroll. Nowadays it is fashionable to display a great many utensils, and to compete in splendor. There is a great difference between the two attitudes of mind. This *tsuru no hitokoe* flower container is said to be treasured by a distinguished family.

*

Ogura *shikishi*: one hundred *shikishi* on which Teika wrote one hundred poems, while living at Mount Ogura near Kyoto

Ise Province: Mie Prefecture at present
"Amanohara": poem by Abe no Nakamaro (701–70): Looking up at heaven above/I see the moon, the very moon/Above Mount Mikasa at Kasuga.
"Yaemugura": poem by the priest Ekei (*ca.* 985): The house in the tangled growth of wild grass/Tells that none come to live here in desolation/But autumn never fails to come round again.
tsuru no hitokoe: lit., "one whoop of a crane," hence a flower container with a long cranelike neck

119. Lord Ryozan

Lord Ryozan was the father of Sammyakuin. In their decline they lived in Satsuma Province. The *kataginu* and *hambakama* were originally designed by Ryozan. They were made by removing the sleeves of the *suo* and adding pleats to it.

*

Ryozan: Konoe Sakihisa (1537–1612), prime minister
Sammyakuin: Konoe Nobutada (1565–1614), government minister and calligraphy master
Satsuma Province: Kagoshima Prefecture at present
kataginu: stiff sleeveless jumper for men's ceremonial wear
hambakama: pleated trousers worn with *kataginu*
suo: men's ceremonial costume

40. Lord Ryozan originally designed the kataginu and hambakama

by removing the sleeves of the ceremonial costume.

120. Footwear

Setta have long been used, and it is said that leather has been attached to the soles since the time of Rikyu. Cotton *tabi* as they are now were first devised by Nagaoka Sansai's mother. She did this because Sansai complained of cold feet when he attended the tea ceremony.

*

setta: leather-soled sandals
tabi: split-toed socks

121. The Hechikan School

There is a school of the tea ceremony called the Hechikan school. It was started by a man named Sakamotoya at Kamikyo in Kyoto, who was fond of the tea ceremony. His tea gatherings were somewhat humorous. His pseudonym was Nyomukan at first, then Hechikan. He was married to Ko Dosan's niece. The Chinese character 丿 *hechi* is the left half of the character 人 "man," so "Hechikan" means that he was one half of a man. He lived a little after Rikyu.

122. The Tea Ceremony with Incense

茶窓閒話

There is a type of tea ceremony using an incense burner. The host rearranges the charcoal and then places an incense burner, an incense container, and chopsticks on a long tray. Before the meal is ready, he brings in the tray and then returns into the kitchen, shutting the *shoji* tightly at the kitchen entrance. The guest of honor appreciates the incense in the burner and brings the incense through his left sleeve into his clothing, keeping it smouldering there. When the incense is burned out, he takes it out through his right sleeve and, retaining the ash, passes the tray to the next guest. The second guest takes another grain of incense from the container and puts it onto the sheet of silver mica in the burner and appreciates the incense, then brings it in through his left sleeve and takes it out through his right. Everything proceeds following the first guest's example until the last guest finishes. One remaining grain of incense is placed on the mica, and the tray is presented to the first guest. He places it at the kitchen entrance for the host. When there are five guests, five grains of incense are placed in the container, and when there are six guests, six grains. The grain of incense is 2 *bu* (6 mm.) square, and about $1\frac{1}{2}$ *bu* (4.5 mm.) thick.

When this ceremony is to be carried out soon after the meal, or when some guest wants to try it, the *shoji* should be kept slightly open. In such cases, only the incense which is lighted at the beginning is appreciated and handed on by each in turn, and then it is returned to the kitchen entrance. It is not necessary that a very fine celadon burner be used, for an old Seto porcelain or another such would do as well. This should be kept in mind. When there is a shelf in the tearoom and incense is burned there, no incense nor scent is to be burned in the hearth.

123. Masterpieces of Calligraphy

A volume of poems written by high priests of Tang China was discovered at an old temple in Iyo Province. It was divided into seven scrolls, and they are now scattered about here and there. Lord Wakizaka has one scroll, and Lord Doi has another. The latter is by the two calligraphers Mao Gulin and Miao Dao. The one that Lord Ii has is a scroll in the style of Teika and his disciples. Fuya Ryosa has another one, done by Chushi.

*

Iyo Province: Ehime Prefecture at present

Mao Gulin: Gulin Qingmao (1262–1329), Chinese Zen priest
Fuya Ryosa: appraiser of old calligraphy
Chushi (1297–1371): Chinese Zen priest

茶窓閒話

124. The Sale of the Unzan

It is in the past fifty years that gold and silver have come to be produced in great quantities in the world. At the end of the Kambun era (1661–73), the Unzan *chaire* possessed by Lord Fukan was requested by Lord Kanamori at a price of one hundred pieces of gold. A certain man heard about this, and said that he would like to buy the tea caddy at that price. But at that time he had only thirty pieces of gold ready, and the remaining seventy pieces were lacking. Indeed there is a large difference between the present world and the past. When he was making a donation to Todaiji temple in Nara, Lord Yoritomo wanted to contribute fifty gold *ryo*, but it was impossible because of the drought that year. This is recorded in the book *Azuma Kagami*.

*

Yoritomo: Minamoto Yoritomo (1199–1246), first shogun of the Kamakura period (1185–1333)
Azuma Kagami: history of the later Kamakura period

125. The Shin Chokusen-shu

When Lord Yusai purchased a copy of the *Shin Chokusen-shu* written by Lord Teika from its possessor, a merchant of Tachiuri in Kyoto, the price was ten pieces of white silver. This was the largest transaction in those days. This book is now said to be treasured by the Karasumaru family.

*

Shin Chokusen-shu: poetry anthology compiled by Teika in 1235

126. Renga Poets

Sogi was a poet who lived more than one hundred forty or fifty years ago. A man named Seian was in charge of serving at the tea ceremony at that time. Once the Old Man met this Seian, who told him how the system of *renga* was formulated and became very popular. Before Sogi it was rare that one hundred poems were fully linked together; they were only recited one after another, he said. The genealogy of *renga* poets is as follows: Shokyu, Shokyu's disciple Joha, Joha's disciple Shoda, Shoda's son-in-law Gensho, Shotaku, Genteki, and Shotei.

127. The Grand Poetry Meeting

The grand poetry meetings at the five great Zen temples of Kyoto were called *tanzaku-giri*. At the time of Nanzenji Den Choro a *tanzaku-giri* was held. Poems were composed on the subject of "The Appreciation of the Snow on Mount Ryosan." Since then no such meeting has ever been held. The procedure of the meeting was as follows: the superior and senior priests of the temples assembled early in the morning and porridge was served. Then each priest wrote down a subject, and handed it round to each of the assembly in turn. The most appropriate one for that day was then chosen. This was called the subject commentary. After the subject had been chosen, it was pasted on the wall above the upper seat. Then paper of a special type was cut into wide strips, and they were stacked up in piles of three strips each. A pile was placed in front of each person in attendance, together with a most beautiful ink stand, writing brush, brush stand, water container, and so on. When a poem was composed, the draft was handed to the members of the assembly in turn. Then it was rewritten in a fair copy. This was placed on a desk in the center of the room, and then one priest from each temple stepped up in turn and recited it. The way of recitation was different in each temple. When the poetry meeting was over, a large dinner party was held. The eating, drinking, singing, and dancing continued until late at night, it is said.

*

five great Zen temples of Kyoto: Tenryuji, Shokokuji, Jufukuji, Jochiji, and Manjuji. Nanzenji temple stood above these five.
tanzaku-giri: lit., "cutting of paper strips"
Nanzenji Den Choro: superior priest *(choro)* of Nanzenji temple

128. The Tosa Diary

A copy of the *Tosa Diary* written by the author, Tsurayuki, himself was preserved as one of the treasures of Rengeo-in temple. Lord Teika copied it and made another book. This was possessed by Genteki, a *renga* poet, and later it was treasured by the Kaga family. It was written mostly in Teika's own handwriting, and only two or three pages at the end had been copied in a handwriting similar in size and shape to Tsurayuki's own. This is mentioned in Teika's afterword, as it was his intention to show an example of Tsurayuki's handwriting to those of later years who would know nothing of it at all. Judging from this, it is clear that samples of Tsurayuki's writing were already very rare even in the age of Teika. It is quite ridiculous that Tsurayuki's writings are often said to be possessed by people here and there. Up to the age of Teika, this book at least of Tsurayuki's must have existed, because its size is mentioned in Lord Teika's book. The Old Man has often seen Teika's book, and found Tsurayuki's style of calligraphy to be rather unique and original. The imitations of today can never bear a resemblance to the original. Teika's book is said to be preserved in the storehouse of a certain lord.

*

Tosa Diary: *Tosa Nikki*, famous diary of a journey from Tosa Province (Kochi Prefecture at present) to Kyoto
Tsurayuki: Ki no Tsurayuki (d. 946), poet
Rengeo-in: temple in Kyoto, now called Sanjusangendo

129. The Bento

In the age of Lord Nobunaga, there was nothing like a lunch box. The first one was made at Azuchi, and it was called a *bento*. There were some people who could not believe that various utensils could be contained in one small box, and said that it was impossible to credit. Nor was there anything like a *hasamibako*. Instead they used *hasamidake*. *Hasamibako* were first made by Lord Tsuda Nagato-no-kami in Osaka.

*

hasamibako: lacquered clothes box for traveling
hasamidake: split bamboo in which clothes were held for traveling

* * *

The several preceding stories may seem to have nothing to do with the tea ceremony, but I dared to write them here in the belief that they, too, might perhaps be of some value.

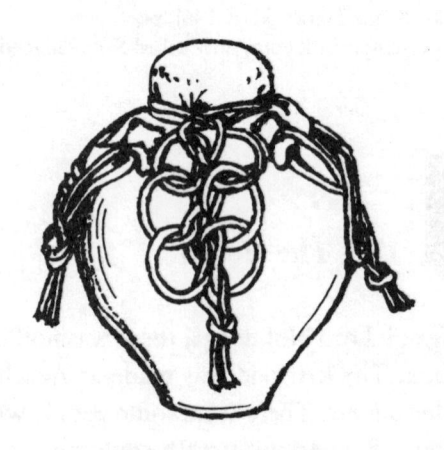

41. A sealed tea-leaf jar.

Afterword to the 1804 edition

WHEN ONE LOVES *material things, one loses one's mind,* *goes an old saying. Lately there have appeared many tea* *connoisseurs who suffer from this thing-loving malaise. They* *should be most thoroughly admonished. This collection of* *anecdotes exceeds all others in that it clearly shows the* *true essence of the tea ceremony. The many stories in this* *book can truly serve as a guide for tea aficionados. They* *tell us of the ideals of the tea ceremony, rejecting especially* *indulgence in material possessions. It so impresses me that I* *have dared to write my sincere appreciation as an afterword* *to this book.*

—MINAMOTO KEICHU

Glossary-Index

Note: Japanese names are presented surname first, except in the case of those individuals commonly known by their given names.

Akechi Hyuga-no-kami Mitsuhide, 80–82, 145
Akechi Samanosuke Mitsutoshi, 80–82
alcove: flower arrangements and containers in, 40–41, 66, 88, 93; scrolls in, 48, 125; size of, 79; tea-leaf jar in, 94
"Amanohara" (poem), 170–71
Ashikaga family, 85. *See also* Yoshimasa
Azuma Kagami (book of history), 177

bag: for *chaire*, 28–30, 74, 106, 160; for *natsume*, 151
basins: in garden, 105; gold, 66–67
bento (lunch box), 181
biwa (Japanese lute), 119

board: for brazier, 54–55; under flower container, 84
Bodhidharma, 61, 118
bondate (preparation of tea on a tray), 104
brazier, 54–55, 91, 142
Buddha, 51, 73, 133–35
Buddhism, 94; Nichiren sect of Zen, 133
Bukkoji temple, 85
Bunka Shurei-shu (poetry anthology), 57

calligraphy: by Chinese priests, 80, 176–77; by Chushi, 176–77; by Daito Kokushi, 126; by Mao Gulin and Miao Dao, 176–77; selection of, 48, 50; by Son'en, 51; by Teika, 126,

[185]

calligraphy *(cont'd)*:
170, 180–81; by Tsuen, 124; by Xitang, 80; by Zen priests, 96–98

chaire (ceramic tea caddies): bag for, 28–30, 74, 106, 160; Gyokudo, 168; *hotei*, 106; *miyako kaeri*, 69–70; Nakayama, 70–73; *nasu (nasubi)*, 106, 108; Seto, 104; Shokokuji, 168–69; Tanemura, 67–69; *utsumi*, 108; *yuto*, 109. See also *katatsuki*

chakabuki (taking tea in turn), 138

chakin (linen cloth for wiping tea bowl), 98–99

charcoal: containers, 59–60, 123; preparation of, 59–60, 62, 74; types and sources of, 62, 119–20

China: calligraphy and paintings from, 80, 96, 176–77; tea plants from, 57; trays from, 110–11; utensils from, 50, 111–12, 139–41, 168

Chojiro, 149–50

clothes, design of, 171–74

daimegamae (type of tearoom), 25–26

daime tatami, 25–26

daisu (table-like stand), 27, 28, 91, 100, 108

Daito Kokushi, 126

Daitokuji temple, 96, 98, 110, 124, 131-32

Dohachi, 61

dobo (tea ceremony master for a nobleman), 85

Emura Sogu (Old Man), 165–66, 168–69, 178, 181

Enshu, Kobori: as agent, 73; opinions and practices of, 46, 74, 89–90, 141; school of, 136; as student of Zen, 97

flower arrangement: for the tea ceremony, 91; harmony, in, 48, 74, 88, 144; by Rikyu, 66–67, 83

flower containers: bamboo, 37–43, 48, 101, 123; basketwork, 84; Gankai, 100; gourd, 48, 100, 118; by Ichio Iori, 118–19; Onjoji, 40–43; *tsuru no hitokoe*, 170–71

fresh-water vessel: of cedar, 123; *efugo*, 80–82; *imogashira*, 146–48

fuga (elegant refinement), 73

fukusa (silk cloth for wiping utensils), 44

Furuori (Furuta Oribe), 136–37, 168

furyu (elegant refinement), 96

Gamo Ujisato, 107–108, 135, 157–58

garden: cleaning of, 63; design of, 104–105; stones in, 104–105, 142–44

Gensho, 178

Genteki, 178, 180

Gyoyo, 138

haikai (informal verse), 124, 126

hearth, 25–26, 51, 59, 100, 176
Hechikan, 93–95, 174
Hideyoshi, Toyotomi: as exemplar, 157, 159; meaning of tea ceremony to, 145; and Rikyu, 37, 40, 53, 66–67, 93, 127–32; utensils of, 53, 121–22, 148
Hokaimon ware, 110
Honganji temple, 111
Hosokawa family, 150. *See also* Sansai; Yusai

Ichio Iori (Ichian), 50, 84, 86, 118–19, 137
Ikenishi Gonsui, 124–26
Imai Sokyu, 40, 136, 148
incense, use of, 107, 153, 165, 175–76
incense burners: *chidori*, 107–108; Tago-no-ura, 153; use of, 175–76
incense containers, 123, 175

Jurakudai palace, 131

kaicha. *See chakabuki*
Kanamori Sowa, 46–49, 137, 177
kataginu (men's ceremonial jumper), 171
Katagiri Sekishu, 137
katatsuki (ceramic tea caddy with protruding shoulders): *enza*, 168–69; Hino, 169; Mozuya, 43–44; *narashiba*, 80–82; *nasu (nasubi)*, 108; Rikyu's practices with, 90, 104, 108, 121; Seto, 104; Unzan, 139–41, 177

Kenninji temple, 45, 112
kettle-lid rests, 36, 116–17
kettle: rings, 36, 84; words for, 90
kettles, types of: Amida-do, 133, 135; Ashiya, 33–34; *daikodo*, 167; *futon*, 36; *hiragumo*, 79–80, 82; Kanto, 34; Kyo, 34; *kikusui*, 167; *otogoze*, 36, 80; *shiribari*, 36; Temmyo, 34; *ubaguchi*, 76–77
Kinoshita Hansuke, 127–30
Ki no Tsurayuki, 180–81
Kissui-in temple, 151
Kitamuki Dochin, 28, 45
kitchen for tearoom, 59, 101, 175–76
kitsuki (cutting off a head), 160
Koan (Tsuda Koheiji), 70–73
Ko Dosan, 94–95, 114, 174
Kogetsu Sogan, 97–98
koicha (thick tea), preparation and serving of, 50–51
koita (small board under brazier), 54–55
koji (honorable title), 123–24
Konoe Sakihisa. *See* Ryozan
Korea, utensils from, 66, 121–22
kuguriguchi (guest entrance of tearoom), 54, 94
Kuroki scroll, 70, 73
Kuze Doku Raisai, 77
Kyogoku Takahiro Anchi, 139–41, 148
Kyoto, tea ceremony of, 90

lantern, stone, 133–35
lacquerers, 31, 110

Makino Sado-no-kami Chikashige, 68–69
Man'yoshu (poetry anthology), 120
Mao Gulin, 176–77
Matsunaga Danjo Hisahide, 79, 82, 145
meibutsu (articles of historical fame): calligraphy, 80; *chaire*, 48, 104, 106, 139–41, 168–69; dagger hilt, 153–54; display of, 151; freshwater vessels, 80, 82; incense burner, 107; *katatsuki*, 43–44, 80, 108, 168; kettles, 34, 80, 167; paintings, 61; tea bowls, 121, 149–50; tea-whisk stands, 113; *temmoku* stands, 112
meisui (good water for tea), 61
Miao Dao, 176
Miidera temple, 41–42
Mozuya Soan, 43–44, 127
Murata Shuko, 25–26, 97
Myokakuji temple, 110
Myorenji temple, 133

Nakao Shinno, 27, 112
Nakao Soami, 85
Nampo Jomyo, 44
Nansoji temple, 116
Nanzenji temple, 180
natsume ("jujube"-shaped lacquered tea caddies): bag for, 151; Konrinji, 151–52; lacquered by Joami, 31; *mentori*, 108; *oshiroidoki*, 58; Rikyu's use of, 31, 58, 90, 108, 123; *seppu*, 108

nijiriguchi (guest entrance of tearoom), 54, 94
Nishikoribe no Hikogimi, 57
Nobunaga, Oda: meaning of tea ceremony to, 145; as military commander and exemplar, 76, 79–80, 145, 157–59; and Rikyu, 32, 37, 121; utensils of, 76, 80–81, 121
Noh plays, 127, 160

Oda Sadaoki, 137, 144
Oda Saemon Yorinaga Nyudo Unjoji, 61
Ogura *shikishi* (calligraphy cards), 170
Okabe Doka, 74
Old Man. *See* Emura Sogu
Old Man's Tales (Rojin Zatsuwa), 166
Osan, 127–31

paintings, 27, 61, 96
poetry. *See haikai; renga; waka*
poetry meetings, grand, 179–80

Raku ware, 48–49, 149–50
renga (linked verse), 85, 132, 165, 178, 180
Rengeo-in temple, 180–81
Rikyu, Sen no: and *chaire*, 28, 30–31, 90, 104, 106, 108, 121, 139–41, 168; charcoal arranged and used by, 59, 62; death of, 132; and disciples, 51, 84, 135–36, 153; education of, 27–28, 46; and family, 30, 40, 107, 127–32,

146; flower arrangements by, 66–67, 83, 91; and flower containers, 37, 40–44, 84, 100–101, 123; garden and tearoom design by, 25–26, 79, 83, 104–105; and Hechikan, 94–95; and Hideyoshi, 37, 40, 53, 66–67, 93, 127–32; house of, 133; and incense and incense utensils, 107, 153; methods of serving tea, 51, 54, 89, 142; and *natsume*, 31, 58, 90, 108, 123, 151; and Nobunaga, 32, 37, 121; on simplicity, 99, 126–27, 151; on sword design, 152–53; and various utensils, 36–37, 50, 123, 133, 142, 146–50; and Zen, 97

Rojin Zatsuwa. See *Old Man's Tales*

Ryozan, 171

Sakamoto Castle, 80–82
Sakamotoya, 174. See also Hechikan
Sakuma Fukan, 135–36, 177
Sakuma Sanekazu, 97–98
Sansai, Hosokawa: as incense master, 153; school of, 136; on sword design, 152–53; as teacher, 118, 156–61; as warrior, 56, 156–61
Sasaki Doyo, 137–38
screen, folding, 100, 170
scroll mounters, 27, 85, 112
scrolls, 70, 73, 91. See also calligraphy; paintings
Seian, 178

Sen family, schools of, 136
Sen no Doan, 54, 79, 170
Sen no Shoan, 40–41, 146
Sensai Sensei, 165. See also Emura Sogu
Sesshu Toyo, 33, 125
Seto ware, 48–50, 104, 176
Shibata Shurinosuke Katsuie, 76–77
Shigi Castle, 79
shikishi (calligraphy cards), 126–27, 170
Shin Chokusen-shu (poetry anthology), 178
Shinjuan monastery, 124–26
Shinnyodo temple, 51
Shoda, 178
shoji (papered sliding door), 83, 175
Shokokuji temple, 168–69
Shokyu, 178
Shotaku, 178
Shotei, 178
Socho, 132, 170
Sogi, 107–108, 170, 178
Sohen, Yamada, 137, 145
Soken, Shinjuan, 124–26
Song dynasty, China, 45
So-on, 30, 107
Sotan, Sen no: on garden and tearoom, 54, 63, 104–105; tea ceremony and utensils of, 58, 138, 142; and Zen, 97, 144–45
suki (aesthetic taste), 77
sukido (pursuit of the tea ceremony), 93, 97
sukisha (expert on the tea ceremony), 88
Sumiyoshiya Somu, 40, 59, 61

[189]

swords, 80; sheath and hilt design of, 152–53

tabi (split-toed socks), 174
Tachibanaya Sogen, 68
Taga Sakon, 137
Taiheiki (book of history), 90–91, 137
Takayama Ukon, 62–63, 135
Takeno Jo-o: articles and utensils of, 55, 100, 170; garden and tearoom of, 25–26, 46, 59, 100; and Zen, 97
Tanabata (Star Festival), 137–38
Tang dynasty, China, 100, 112, 141, 176
tankei (oil lamp), 30, 77
tanzaku-giri (grand poetry meetings), 179–80
tea, distinguishing types of, 137
tea bowls: *hachihiraki*, 133, 135, 150; Ido, 121–22; Ki Miidera, 70, 73; Raku ware, 48–49, 149–50; *temmoku*, 51, 99, 113; *totoya*, 66; Tsutsui, 121–22
tea caddies. See *chaire*; *katatsuki*; *natsume*
tea ceremony: food of, 78, 142; harmony and contrast in, 46–48, 62–63, 74; with incense, 175–76; at Kyoto and Sakai, 90; methods of performing, 48, 50–52, 89–90, 138; nature of, 77–78, 144–45; schools of, 84, 136–37, 174
tea-leaf jars: opening of, 41, 142; *matsubo*, 53; placement of, 94; *rengeo*, 168–70
tea plants, growing of, 57
tearoom: construction and orientation of, 25, 41, 45, 79; entrance of, 54, 94; garden's relation to, 46, 86, 88, 93, 144; made from Rikyu's house, 133; shelf of, 151, 176; use of utensils in, 99, 108, 146; words for, 54. See also alcove; hearth
tea scoops, 86, 114–16, 119, 123; makers of, 116
tea whisk, 66
tea-whisk stands, kinds of: *hasami-chawan*, 114; Shinno, 113
Teika, 120, 126, 176, 180–81
temmoku bowls, 51–52, 99, 100, 111–12
Temmyo kettles, 34
Todaiji temple, 177
Togano-o temple, tea grown at, 57, 137
Tosa Diary (Tosa Nikki), 180–81
Toyobo Chosei, 51–52, 149
Toyokuni shrine, 83
Toyo manner of serving tea, 52
trays: origins of, 110–11; *uchiaka*, 110–11; use of, 104, 151, 175
Tsuda Sokyu, 121, 136
Tsuen, 124–26
Tsuji Yojiro, 34

Uraku, Oda: as disciple of Rikyu, 135; opinions of, 62;

[190]

school of, 136; utensils of, 44, 111, 114, 148
usucha (thin tea), preparation and serving of, 51–52
utensils, tea ceremony: handling of, 74; selection of, 50. See also *meibutsu*

wabi (simple taste), 98–99
wabicha (simple tea ceremony), 119–20
wabisuki (moderate experts in the tea ceremony), 51–52, 55, 116
waka (thirty-one syllable verse), 165–66

water for tea, 59, 95

"Yaemugura" (poem), 170–71
yocha. See *chakabuki*
Yoshimasa, Ashikaga, 27, 77
Yoshiro. *See also* Sen no Rikyu
Yusai, Hosokawa, 70, 73, 107, 122, 178
Yujian, 27

Zen Buddhism, 96–98, 144, 157
Zenkyo-an monastery, 112
Zen temples, five great, 179–80